COLLECT PRINT COLLAGE

Printing with Nature

SUE BROWN

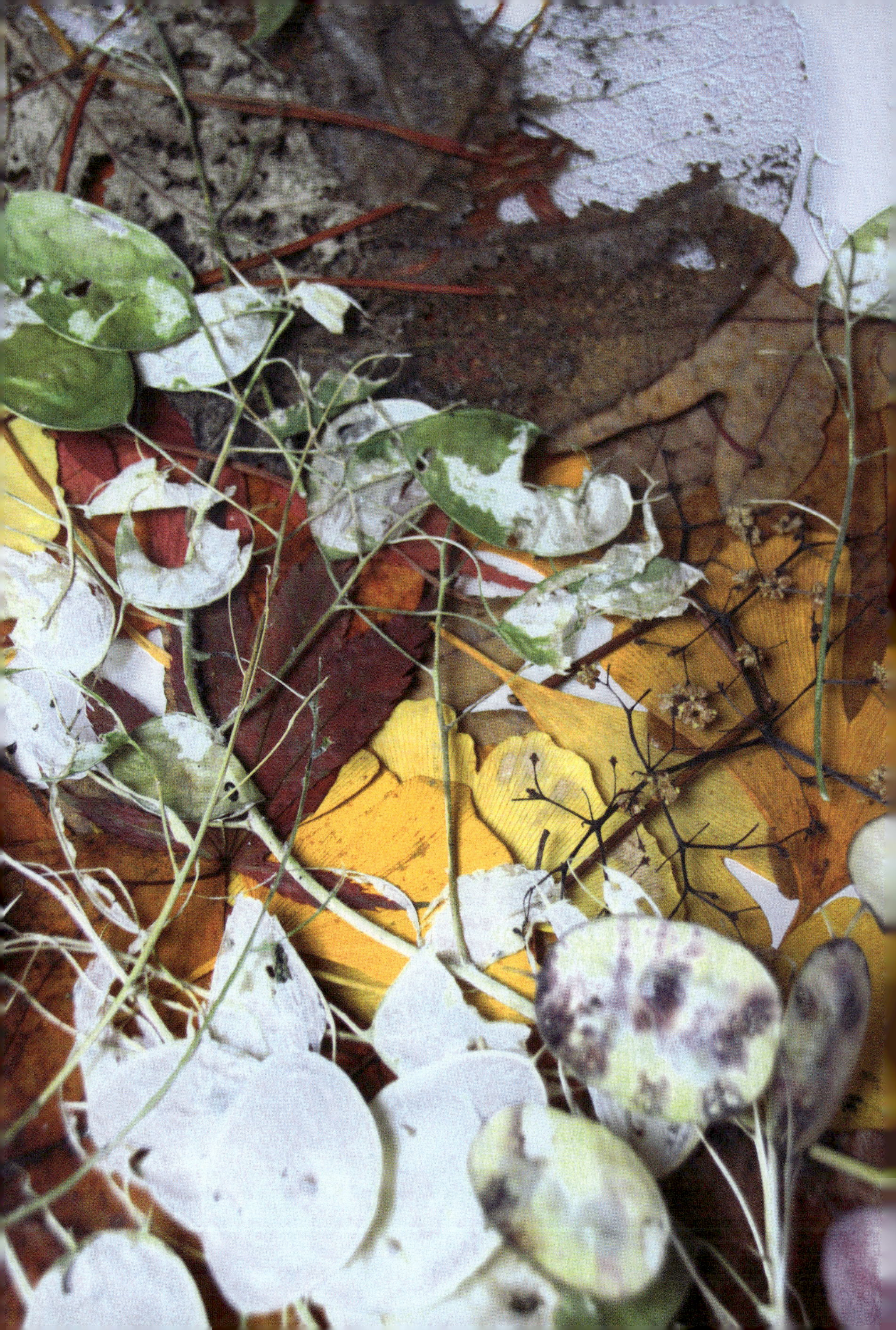

COLLECT PRINT COLLAGE

Printing with Nature

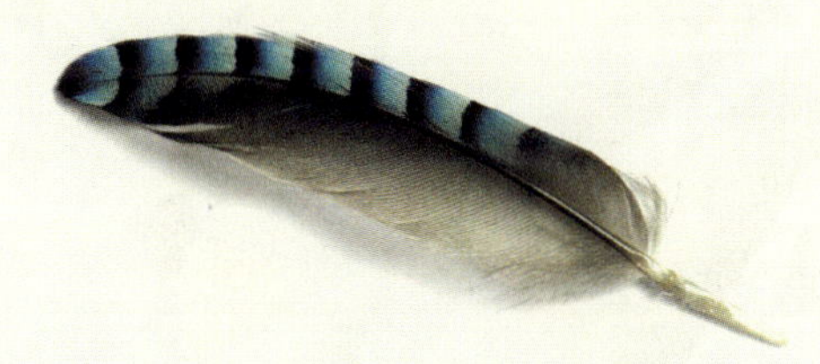

SUE BROWN

CONTENTS

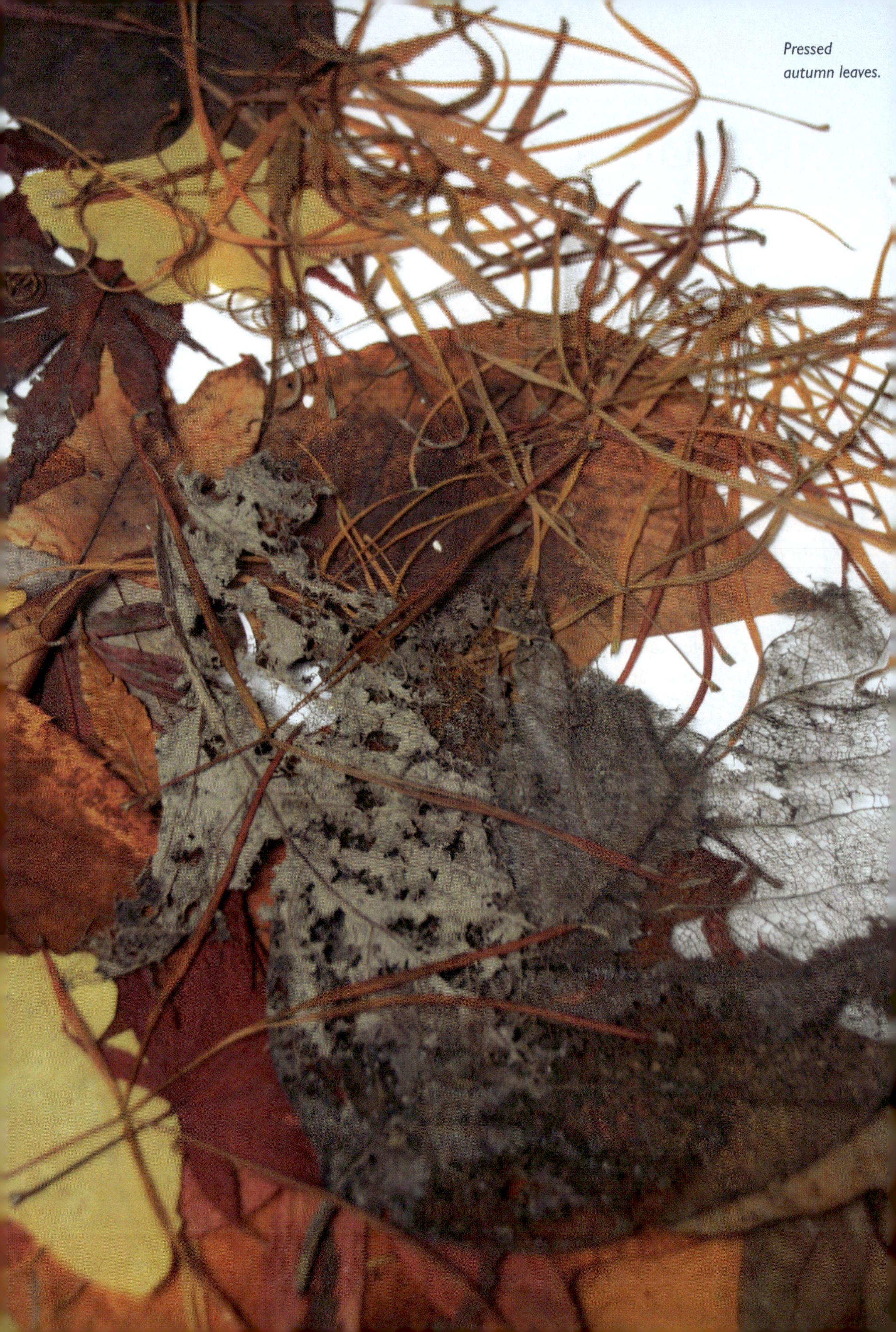

Pressed
autumn leaves.

INTRODUCTION

Yutori (Japanese for space or margin): intentionally to slow down to savour the world around us, taking time to appreciate nature, to reflect and find balance in our lives; spaciousness.

I n this fast-paced world, we often yearn to slow down and find quiet space in our lives. More and more of us are looking for that space in the natural environment and it is now widely accepted that being in and connecting with nature makes us feel better, both physically and psychologically. A long walk in the countryside, a stroll in the local park or simply sitting in a garden all help us to re-charge, while bringing the outside in – through photographs and drawings or collections of leaves, feathers, stones and shells – connects us to the great outdoors, when we are back at home.

Cyanotype on a botanical contact print using the same shaped leaf monoprinted.

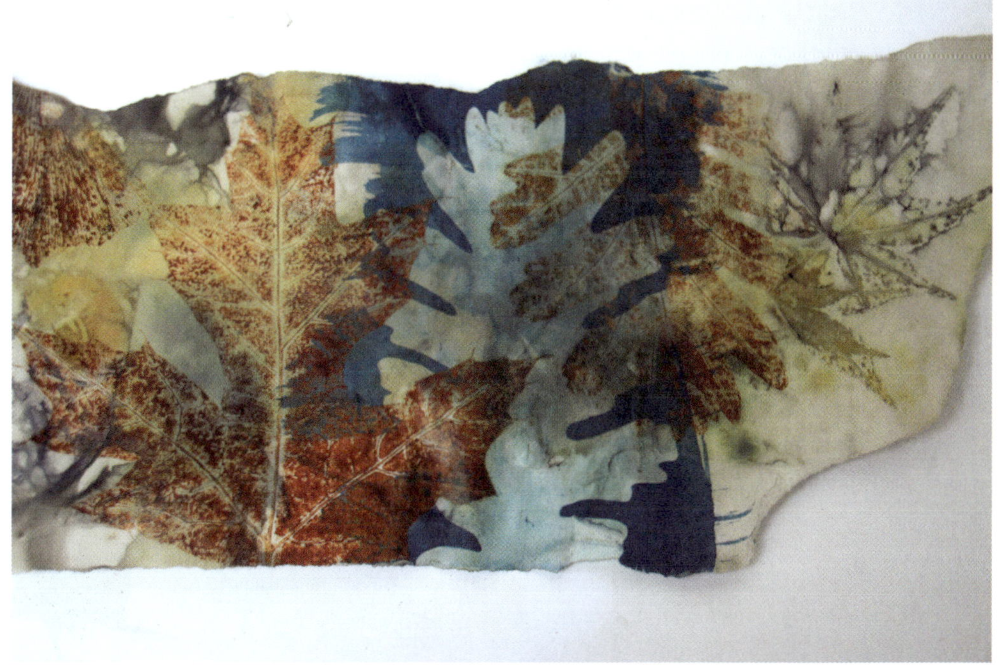

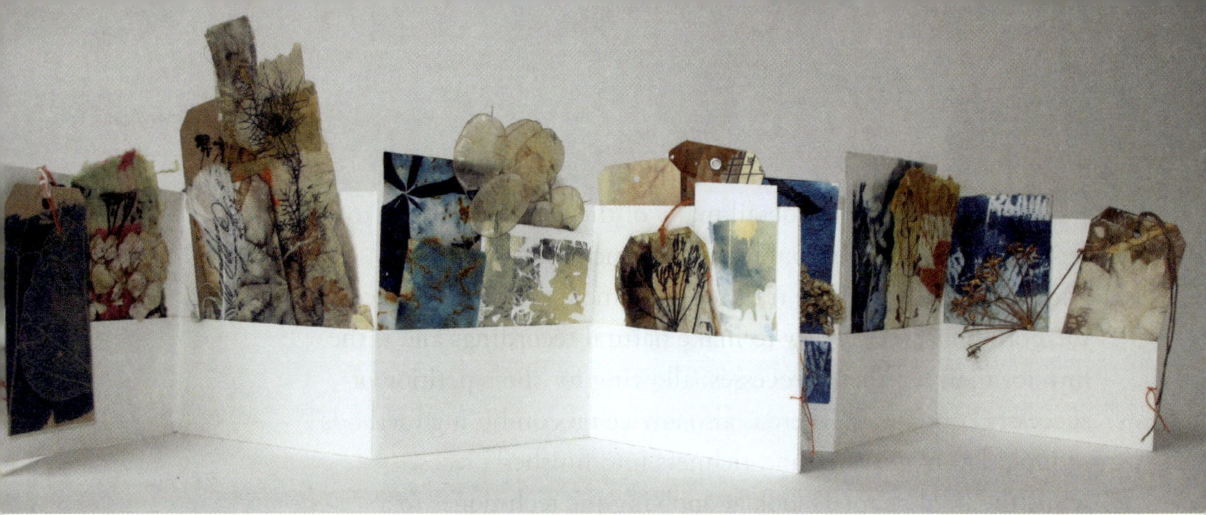

As an artist, I am inspired by nature as much as process. I am stimulated by the natural world for my own satisfaction and want to capture its beauty. I record my encounters with birds and my activities on the allotment and in my garden through sketchbook drawings and printmaking. But I do not just draw birds, flowers and leaves; I like to work directly with natural things, collating collections and making marks on paper with the resources I gather.

Many of the processes I use are only possible at specific times of year. Prints made with cyanotype (a Victorian photographic technique that uses natural light to expose an image), for example, require summer sunshine, while my botanical contact prints are created from particular plants growing in my garden or the hedgerows. (Botanical printing is a technique used to print leaves and flowers directly onto paper and fabric using heat and moisture to transfer pigments.) This requires patience and a sensitivity to time and place, but it also means that much of my practice is seasonal and connected to the rhythm of the natural world.

Displaying completed collages in a concertina pocketbook.

HOW TO USE THIS BOOK

Collect, Print, Collage aims to demonstrate how creativity can be sparked by looking at the world around us and how the wonders of nature can be captured through interesting and satisfying artistic processes.

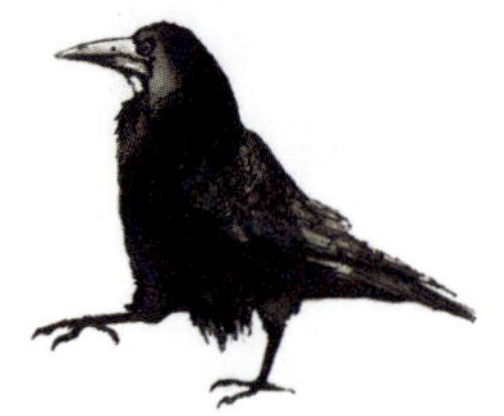

The pages that follow detail many of the techniques I use to record the natural environment that I encounter day to day. Simple printmaking (the transfer of pigment from one surface to another) is an easy way to make natural recordings and is the link for many of these processes, allowing for the repetition of successful outcomes. There is also advice on combining methods to build layers, textures and richness into finished pieces, while the final chapters look at applying the techniques to a sketchbook practice and simple artist's book-making forms.

This is a book for both artists with an existing creative practice and those new to producing a visual record of the world around them. The techniques are suitable for most creative abilities and one or two may already be familiar to some readers. Lists of the materials and equipment required are provided, along with step-by-step guides and support if things go slightly differently than expected. There are also creative extensions for those interested and confident with the processes.

Interspersed throughout the projects are personal essays by three artists I particularly admire; Tara Axford, Louise Richardson and Jill Walker.

Botanical contact print with bird-shaped mask.

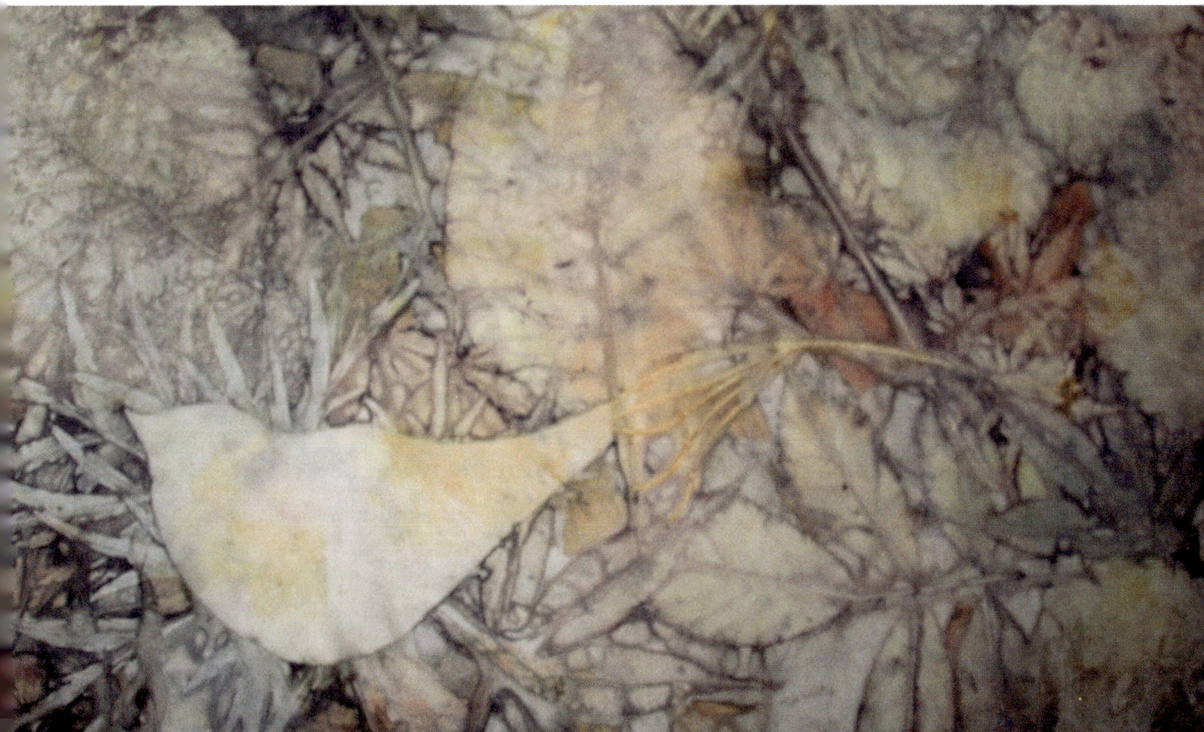

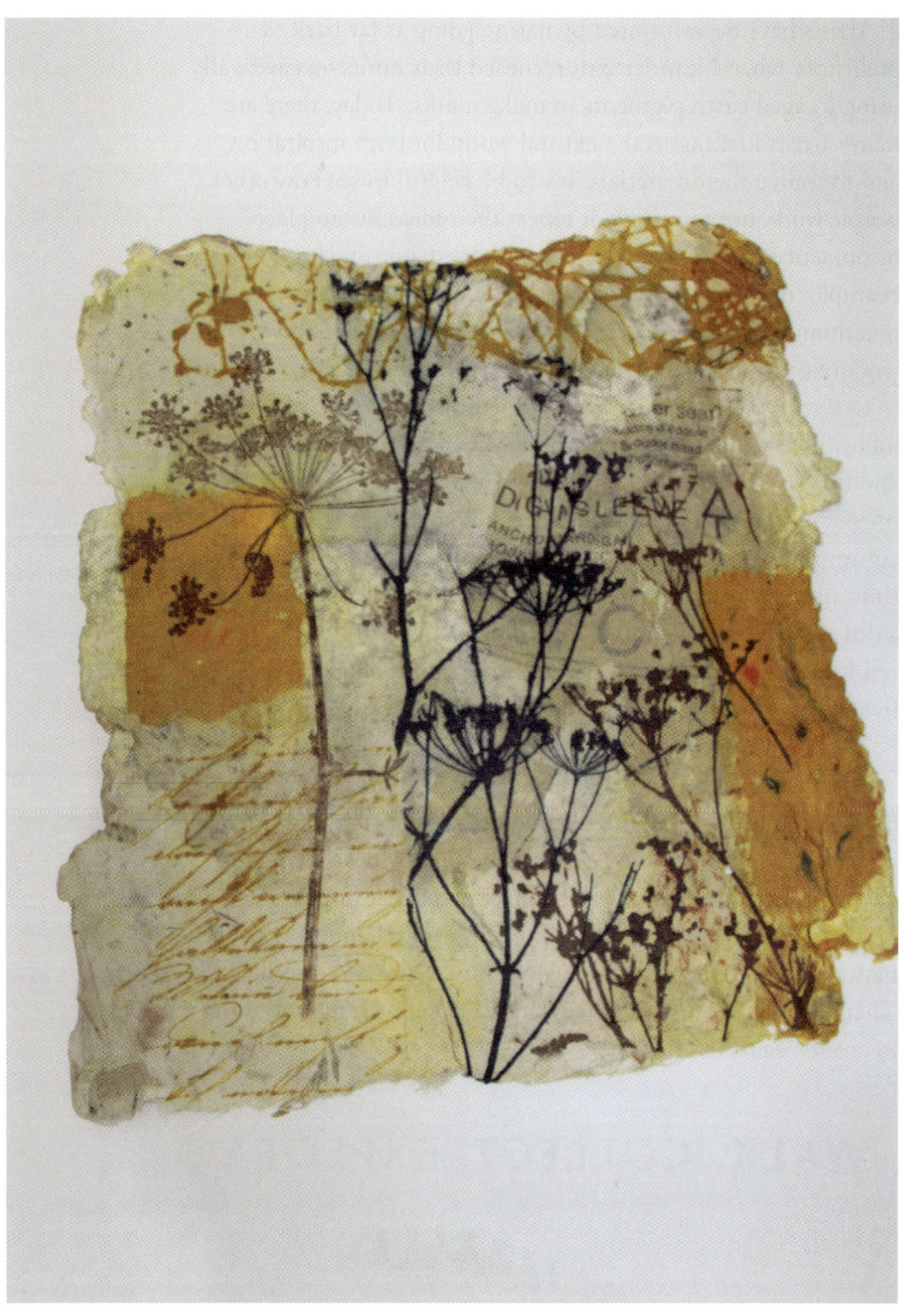

Monoprinting across joomchi.

Artists have been inspired by nature going as far back as prehistory when Neanderthals recorded their hunts on cave walls using foraged earth pigments to make marks. Today, there are many artists looking to the natural world for both inspiration and to source their materials. It can be helpful to see how other people work, not to mimic or repeat their ideas but to place our practice within a creative community. Choosing just a few examples immediately feels like a rejection of other interesting practitioners, but introducing these few will be a gateway to the work of other artists working closely with nature.

Collect, Print, Collage can be worked through systematically, following the seasons as they unfold – making marks with leaves and flowers as they appear in springtime, creating cyanotype images in high summer, using leaves to monoprint with in the autumn – but there are no hard and fast rules; enthusiasm, time and energy are the best leads. Techniques can be used in a different order – cyanotype in winter sun will give a different result; plants in spring will not yield the same colours as those in autumn. Everything found here is intended to be a starting point for personal enquiry and other creative projects.

The book may become part of your regular creative practice, or you might simply dip in when it feels appropriate and time is available. But however you use it, I hope the ideas it contains add another dimension to your collecting habits, inspire you to try out some of the techniques and help you to connect with the natural world. After all, if being in nature restores our wellbeing, what could be more restorative than working with natural things to create beautiful artifacts?

WALK, COLLECT, EXPLORE

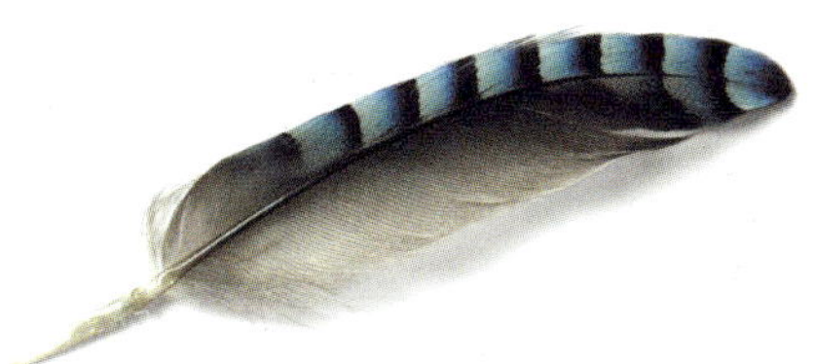

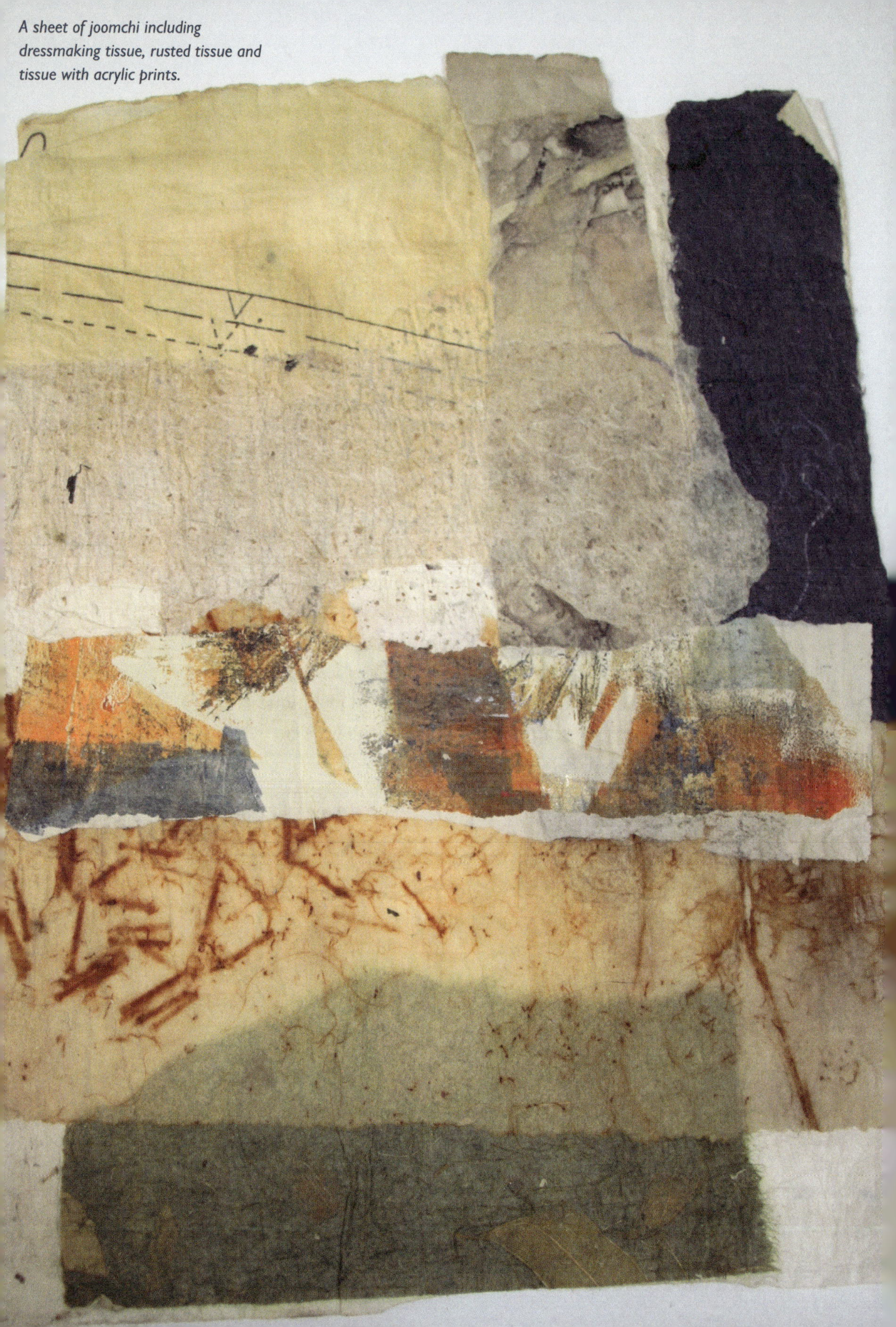

A sheet of joomchi including dressmaking tissue, rusted tissue and tissue with acrylic prints.

CHAPTER 1

CREATING NATURAL SURFACES

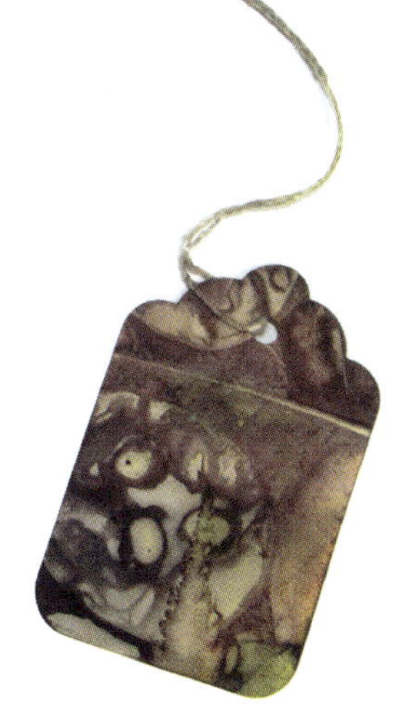

Werifesteria – to wander longingly through the woods in search of mystery and magic.

BOTANICAL CONTACT PRINTING

Also known as 'eco' printing, botanical contact printing is a basic process that uses heat and moisture to release natural pigments from leaves and flowers. At its simplest, it can be used to transfer the patterns, textures and colours of leaves and flowers onto paper and fabric. And it is a wonderful technique to capture the spirit of the season, record a favourite walk or document the progress of a garden or allotment.

Layers of wire wool, onion skins, black elder and rose leaves.

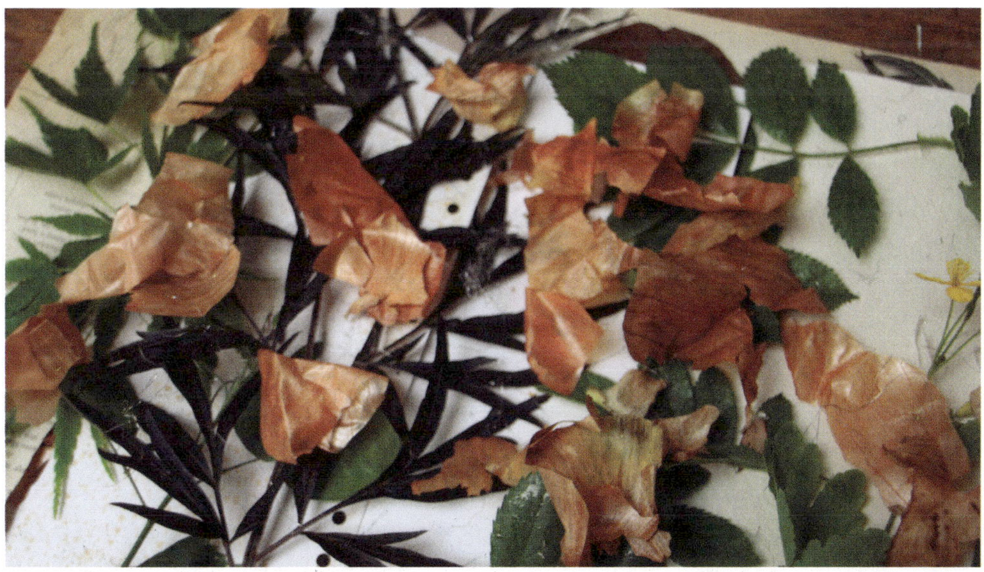

Botanical contact printing is an addictive procedure and, once mastered, can produce a stockpile of resource material to use in future projects. But this comes with a warning: some pieces will be just too lovely to want to cut up and use! As with all these apparently simple processes, there are a few tips and tricks to help you achieve the best possible results.

Collecting vegetation

It does not take long to amass enough vegetation to make a series of botanical contact papers – I often return from a walk with a collection of leaves I have gathered, attracted by their shapes and colours. I do not encourage plundering the countryside of its flowers and plants – care and thoughtfulness should be applied when harvesting resources. Pick windfall material off the ground, or take only where there is an abundance of growth. Gardening gloves will prevent scratches – just because things are natural it does not mean they are clean or non-toxic. A pair of secateurs is useful too, to prevent branches being ripped out of the hedgerows.

Gardens are a good place to collect – either your own or, with permission, someone else's. Gardens need constant taming, so are a good supply of botanical resources.

A glorious autumn red.

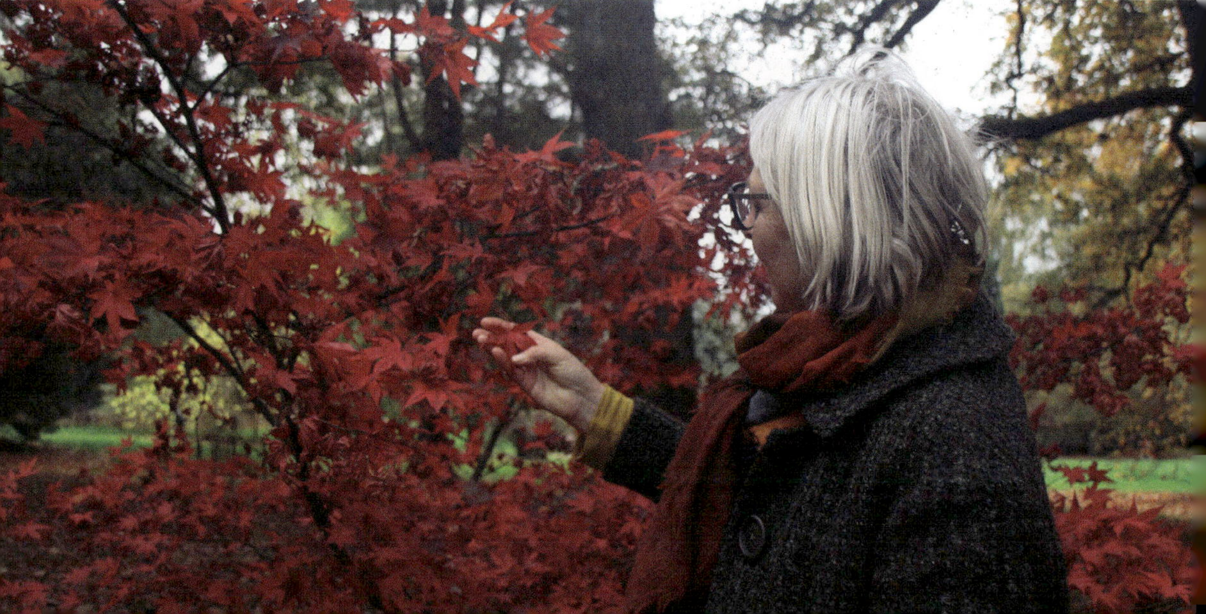

The middle of summer is probably the best time to collect, but different plants that work well for botanical contact printing will appear at other points of the year. I find myself making botanical contact paper in the late spring and throughout the summer as that is when my favourite plants are about, especially in the garden.

Like many natural things, finding the best leaves and flowers to use is trial and error. The seasons, weather and the printing surface will all affect the result. Different tannin levels are found naturally in leaves at different times of year, this acts as a mordant affecting the colour produced in a print.

Here is a list of vegetable matter that works particularly well, but it is by no means definitive. Everyone has their favourite plant that gives them the result they are looking for.

From a walk:	From the garden:
Blackberry leaves	Smoke bush leaves (cotinus)
Oak leaves	Acer leaves
Wild rose leaves	Rose leaves
Fern leaves	Sambucus nigra leaves and flowers
Greater celandine plants	Passion flower
Walnut leaves	Geranium flowers and leaves
Alder leaves	Marigold flowers
	Cosmos flowers

The list could be endless but these have all proved to work well and, with the addition of a collection of onion skins, both orange and red, you can produce beautifully colourful papers. The dried onion skins can be collected over time and stored but flowers and leaves should be used as soon as possible after gathering. Leaves and flowers that have been picked and not kept in water will lose their shape.

Gather together all you need to start a botanical contact print.

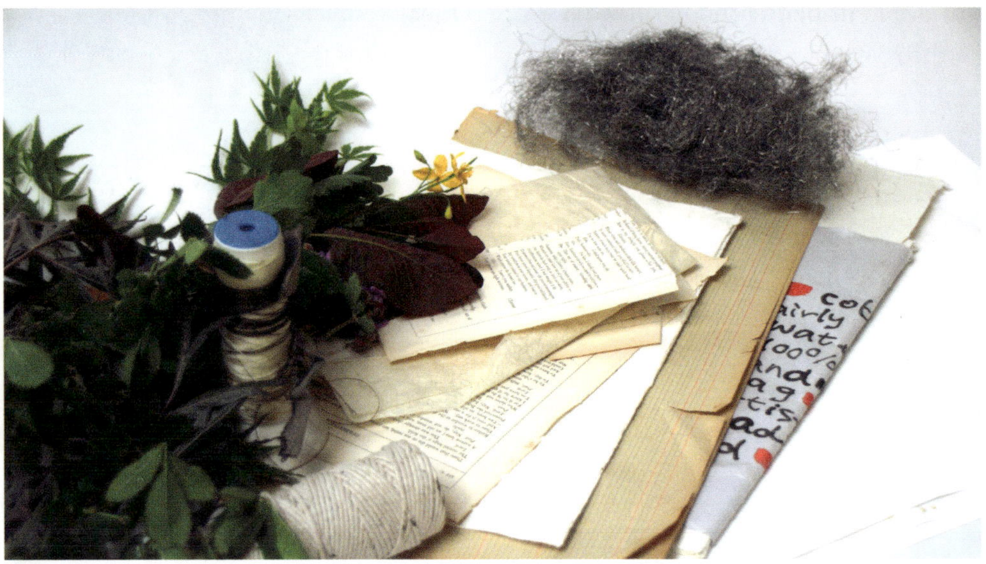

Equipment

- Large cooking pot. The pot should not be used for anything other than botanical contact printing
- Sink waste pipe cut slightly smaller than the pot. Suitable piping can be found in DIY stores
- Hot plate or the cooker in a well-ventilated kitchen
- Tongs
- Rubber gloves

Materials

- Flowers, leaves and onion skins
- Coarse wire wool
- String or strong linen thread
- White vinegar
- A variety of papers: cartridge of differing weights; wet strength tissue; newsprint; old book papers

Gathering everything together before starting will make the process easier

Boiling and printing

1 Use a large, rusted cooking pot that is only used for this purpose. Cut several pieces of sink waste pipe, making certain they fit easily into the pot. This can be done with a hack saw. Having a few pipes available means you can fit a batch of prints into one boil.

2 Cut or rip a variety of paper types the same width as the sink pipe. (The strips can be longer than the pipe, but not wider.) If you want to make more than one print at a time, roll a couple of strips around the pipe.

3   Have all the onion skins, leaves and flowers ready to hand to make up the rolls.

4   Fill the pot with water (if you want to speed the process up, use pre-boiled water) and pour in a glug of white vinegar. This does not need to be a precise amount. The vinegar acts as a mordant encouraging the paper to take on the patterns and colour of the plant.

5   Bring the water to simmering point.

Layering your finds

1   Lay the first length of paper out flat. Wearing rubber gloves, pull out the coarse wire wool and sprinkle sparsely over the surface. Follow with a scattering of onion skins, then arrange the leaves and flowers. Lay the leaves vein-side up for the best patterns. The more material layered, the busier the pattern.

2   Now, place another strip of paper over the layer of leaves, onion skin and wire wool. Experiment by using a variety of smaller pieces of paper rather than one sheet. Try different weights of cartridge, rag paper or pages from old books. This will create many paper samples to use later.

Two or three layers per bundle is optimal as too many layers and too much vegetation affects the contact between leaves, paper and plastic pipe.

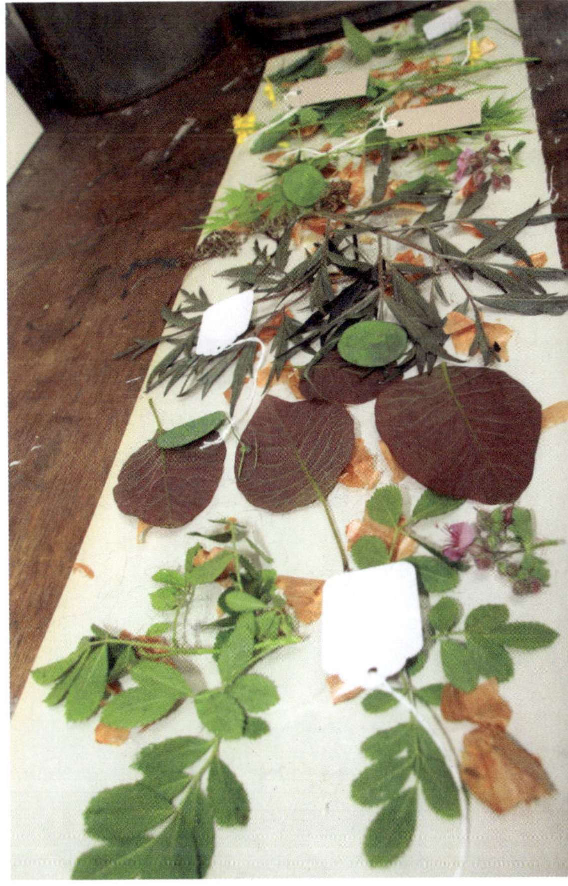

Lay out leaves and flowers on wire wool and onion skins on base paper, vein side up.

Lay selected papers on top of vegetation.

Create samples using different papers for the top layer. For example vintage book papers and cartridge paper.

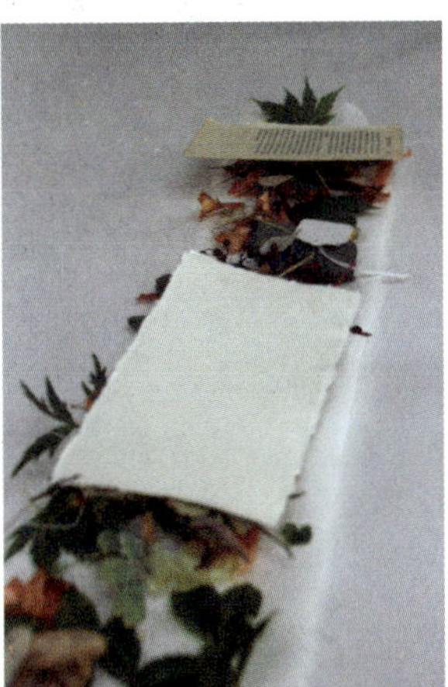

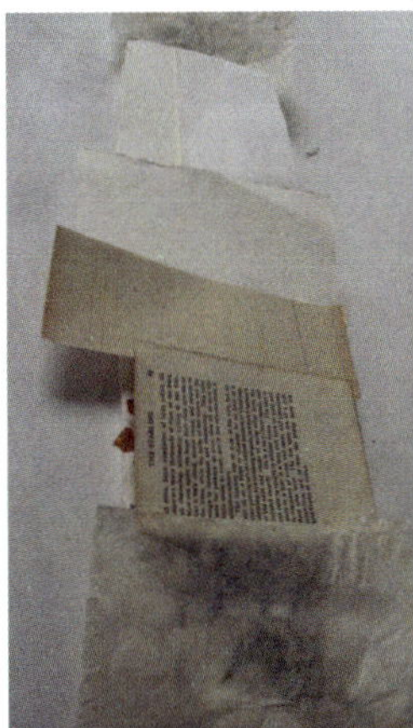

Making the bundles

1   Cut a good length of string or strong linen thread and have it to hand. Overestimate how much you need as running out mid-tying is awkward.

2   Take the pipe and, starting at one end of the paper, roll the paper up around the outside of the pipe, making sure the roll is tight. It is the tight contact between vegetable matter, paper and pipe that will make for a successful and detailed print. Ensure that the roll is straight – if the paper starts to veer off beyond the edge of the pipe the roll may no longer fit the pot.

3   Starting from the centre of the roll, wind the string/thread securely from one end to the other and tie firmly back in the middle. You can make as many bundles as can be fitted into the pot but keep in mind that boiling lots of bundles together will change the colour of the water. To ensure bright colours, boil the bundles in smaller batches using clean water and vinegar.

4   Pop all the bundles into the pot of simmering vinegar and water, ensuring that all the bundles are covered by the water. Boil for at least an hour.

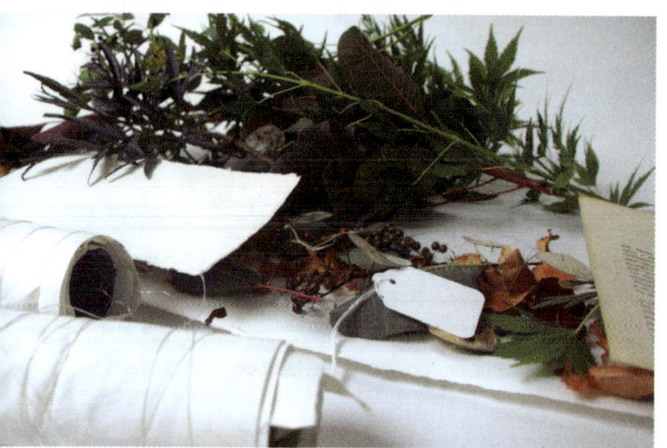

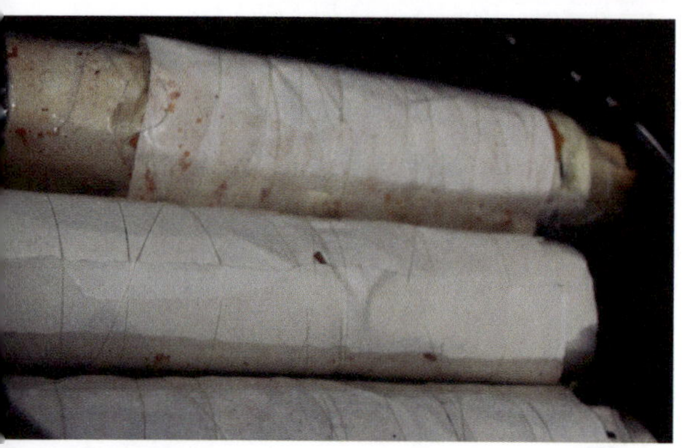

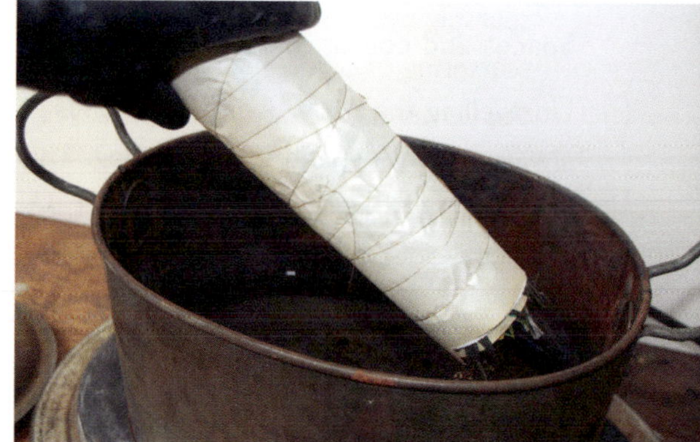

Roll everything together very tightly. Make as many rolls as the pot will take comfortably.

Pop the rolls into simmering water containing a splash of vinegar.

Boil bundles for about an hour.

5   When the time is up, remove the bundles from the water with tongs. Cut the binding and carefully unroll the paper. Wet paper can be fragile, so gently ease the papers apart and pick off the unwanted boiled vegetation.

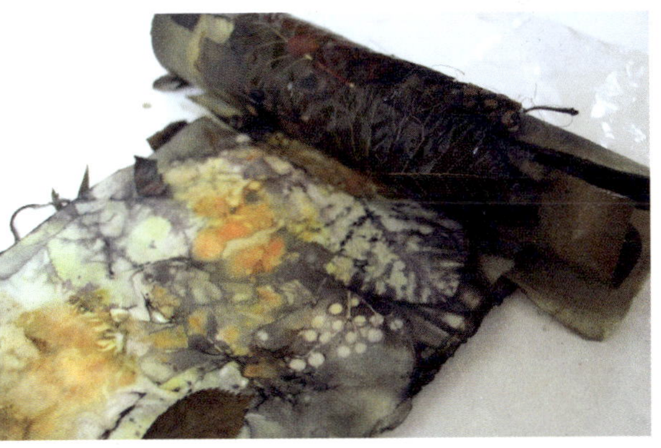

Carefully unroll the bundles, wet paper can tear easily.

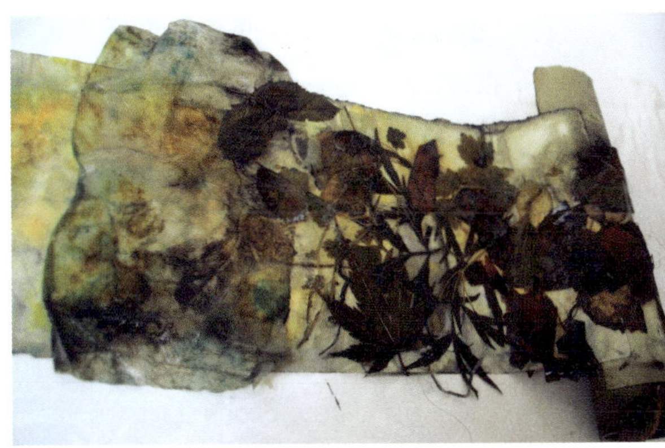

Take extra care if the bundle unrolls upside down.

Spaces and colour

Unravelling the paper from each roll is always surprising, and often thrilling. The carrier sheet that takes the first layer of wire wool and onion skin will always take on a different look to the facing paper placed on top of the leaves.

It is tempting to throw everything onto the surface, but with more than one pipe cut to fit the pot and several pieces of paper prepared, it might be interesting to try just using onion skins in a bundle, or one type of leaf. However, the only element I would not change is the sprinkling of wire wool onto the carrier sheet as, with the vinegar, it acts as a mordant and encourages the plant matter to give up its colour.

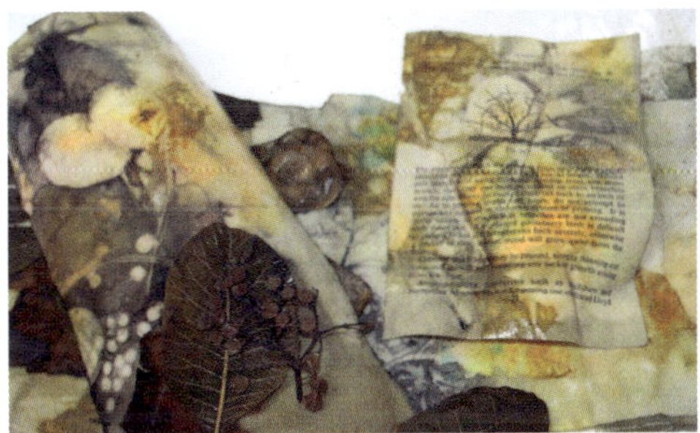

Different papers will take the plant prints with varied intensity.

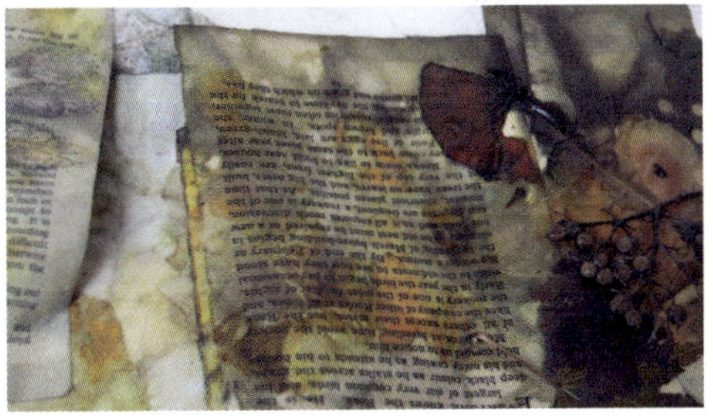

Vintage book pages take the leaf and flower prints strongly.

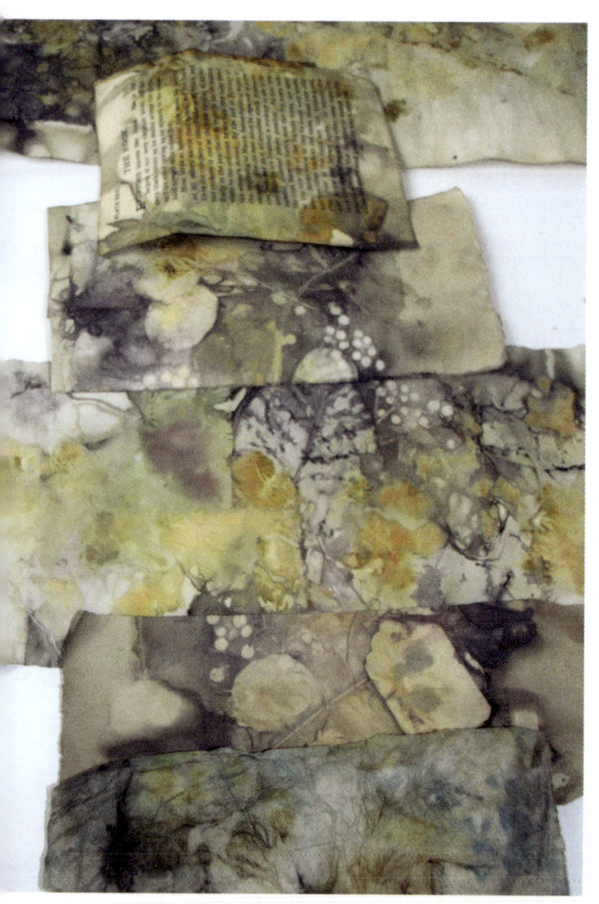

Sampling different papers will indicate which paper works well for specific projects.

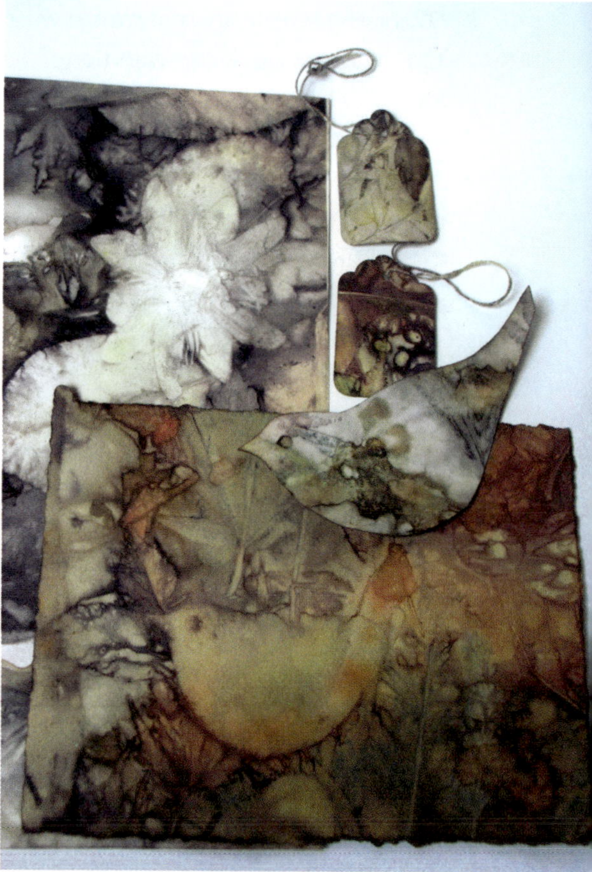

Experiment with adding paper shapes and labels. They will act as masks on the botanical print.

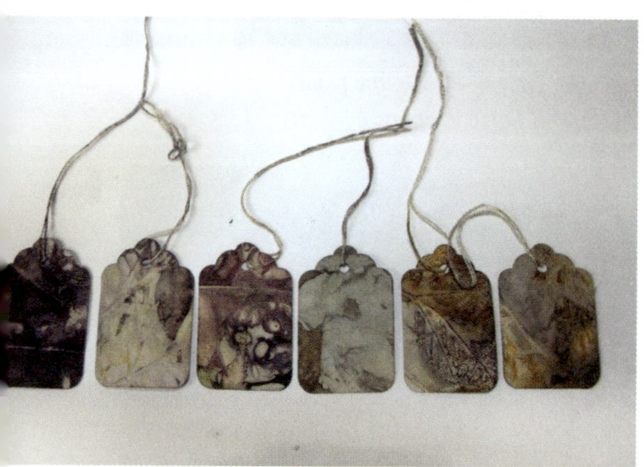

Including labels in the bundle during the boil will create delicious small prints.

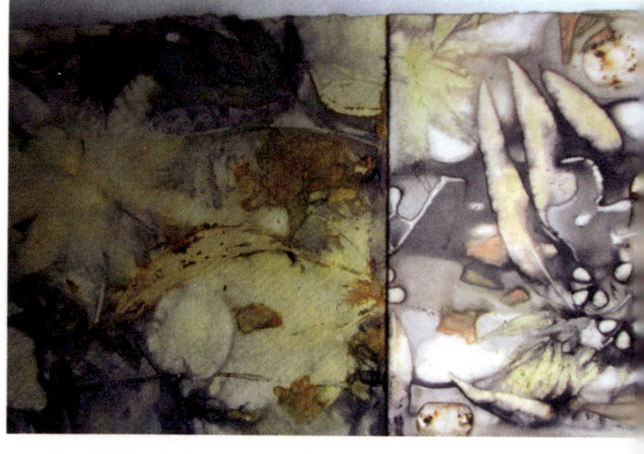

Textured paper will create a different edge to a print than smooth cartridge.

It is possible to create areas of calm in what can be the hectic looking composition produced by botanical contact printing. Add a graphic element to a natural surface with cut shapes. Using cartridge paper, cut simple or complex shapes and lay them onto the leaf layer before covering with the facing paper. Ensure that the bundle is securely and tightly rolled before boiling for an hour. The paper shapes act as a resist, leaving blank spaces on the receiving paper where further drawing, note taking or printmaking can be introduced.

Health and safety

- Just because things are natural, it does not mean they are safe. Some plants are poisonous and should be handled with care when picking and during the boiling process.

- Use gloves to handle wire wool as it can cause very nasty cuts when teasing it apart and sprinkling it onto the carrier paper.

- Avoid putting the boiled leaves onto the compost heap as they are full of wire wool fragments, which will change the acidity of the compost.

- Extra care should be taken with boiling water. Use tongs to lift bundles in and out of the very hot pot.

- Boil the pot in a well-ventilated room.

- Do not over fill the pot with the bundles as this will make the boiling water overflow.

- When unbundling the boiled rolls, be aware that the moisture from the roll is a dye and will stain work surfaces. Unravel prints on a plastic sheet with a cloth to hand.

Once this process is mastered, it produces very rewarding results on most papers and natural-fibre fabrics such as silk and wool. The prints will leave a reminder of that walk, or memory of those precious plants in a garden.

CYANOTYPE

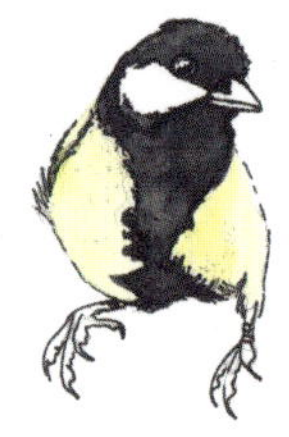

The camera-less photographic process of cyanotype works by coating paper or fabric with iron salts, then placing a mask, object or stencil over the infused surface and exposing it to UV light. Detailed images can be made predominantly in a vivid cyan blue. The process is both spontaneous and satisfying and takes advantage of being outside on a summer day.

Cyanotype was discovered by scientist and astrologer, Sir John Herschel in 1842. Herschel worked closely with pioneering photographer William Henry Fox Talbot and between them they created a stable formulation that we still use today. The process is very much where science meets art and the collaboration of Talbot's photographic developments and Herschel's in-depth knowledge of chemistry led to the work of Anna Atkins who, in 1843, became the first person to produce books using photographic images. Atkins, a friend of the Herschel family, used the cyanotype process to take photographic impressions of British algae and created thousands of cyanotype prints, self-publishing around 26 volumes.

From left to right. Cyanotype on map paper. Music score and toned. A double exposure.

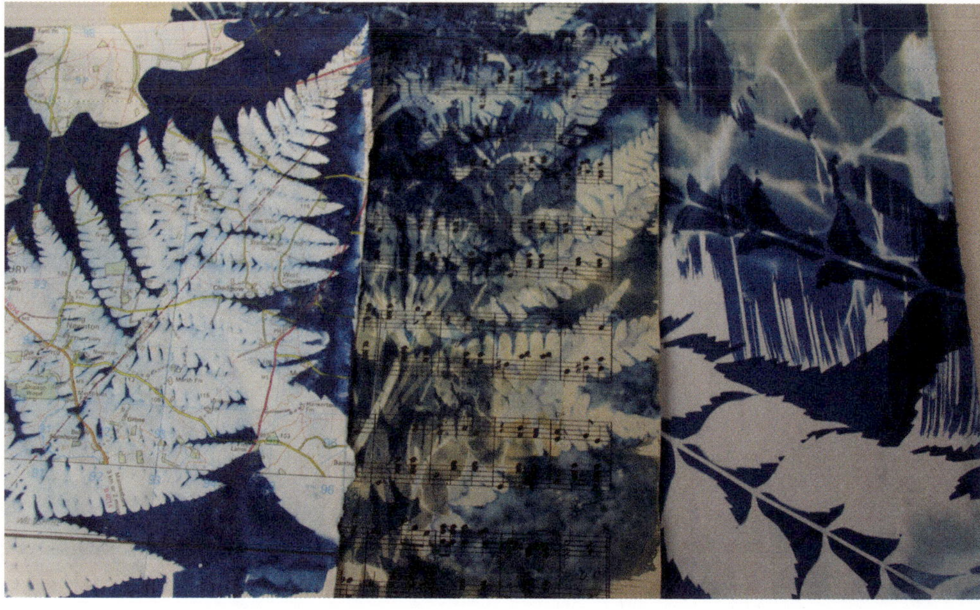

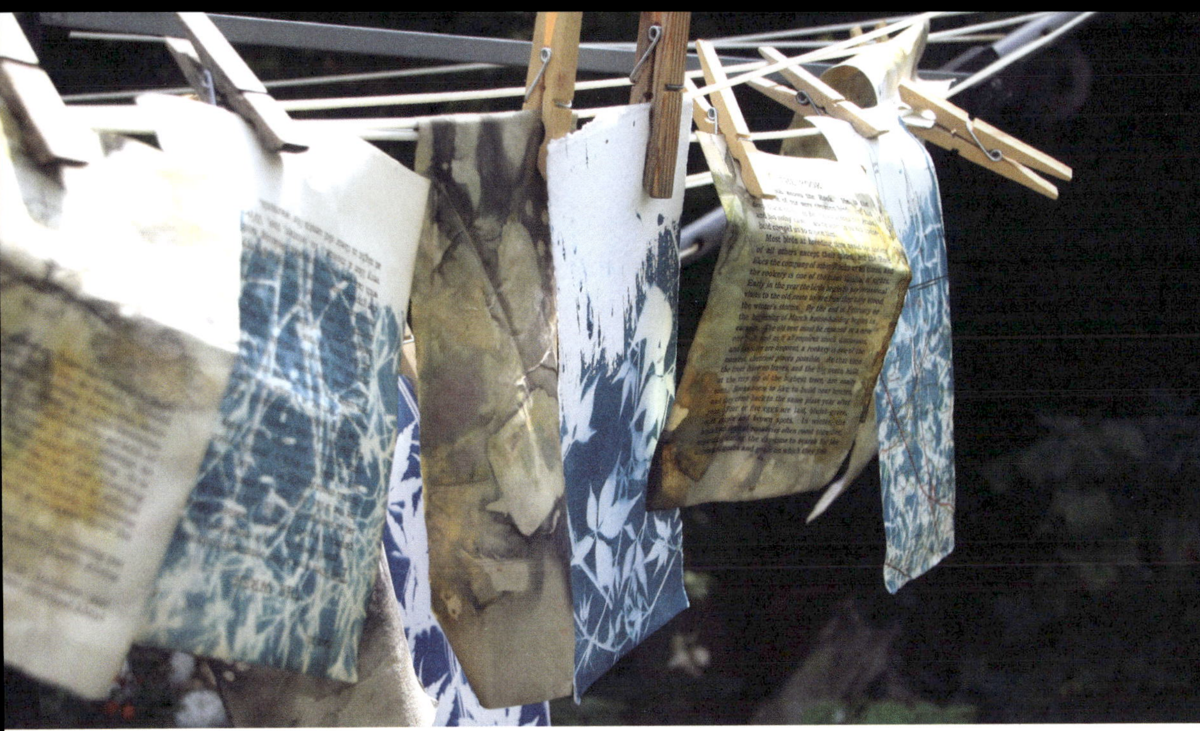

Drying cyanotypes and botanical contact prints.

These works are an early contribution to the art of botanical illustration. After Herschel's death in 1871, the process became a commercial success as a way of copying engineering diagrams and architectural drawings, hence the name 'blueprint'.

Cyanotype printing is an intriguing and compelling way of working. There is a simplicity in a process that requires nothing more than sunlight, water and a couple of chemicals. Once the surface is coated with the mix of the two chemicals, it is simply a matter of laying down leaves, flowers or even found objects and exposing them to the sun. The resulting image is also called a photogram. The chemicals used in this process are ferric ammonium citrate and potassium ferricyanide – I use a ready prepared kit which makes the chemistry of this process easier for anyone new to the technique.

Inspiration can come from fresh, newly-foraged materials or from a collection of flowers and leaves picked some time ago then pressed, dried and stored. I rarely have time to process my finds as soon as I come back from an outing, so I pop them between kitchen towels or tissues and place them under a heavy book to use later. (I talk about pressing and drying later in the book, see p69.) Whatever the method chosen, cyanotype is a simple and effective way to record the natural world.

Gathering everything together before starting will make the process easier.

Equipment

- Several A4 glass clip frames
- Bulldog clips
- Bucket or tray
- Large sponge applicators
- Rubber gloves
- Black photographic grade plastic bags
- Jar with a screw-top lid

Materials

- Cyanotype sensitiser kit – the chemicals in these starter kits are pre-measured making them easy to use and they come with clear mixing instructions. There are many starter kits on the market, but the Jacquard Cyanotype Sensitiser kit (available from specialist art suppliers) is a good place to start. The unused chemicals keep well in a dry place and the instructions to mix parts A and B are clear and easy to follow.
- A variety of papers – cartridge of differing weights; wet strength tissue; newsprint; old book papers.
- Grasses, leaves flowers, objects – anything you'd like to record.
- Soda ash, also known as sodium carbonate and often used as washing soda.
- Green and black tea; coffee; red wine.

Mixing the chemicals

I have been making cyanotype prints for several years and always use the kits with the ready-measured formula. (They save you having to buy the chemicals separately and mean you don't need to measure out the right proportions, which requires a set of scales.) These instructions assume you are using a kit. Although they are safe, do follow the instructions and wear gloves.

1 Mix parts A and B according to the instructions in the kit, then measure out the required solution into a screw topped jar.

2 Place the jar in a light-proof black plastic bag ready to use. The instructions on the kit will lead you to believe that, when mixed, the chemicals will last 2–3 hours but you can stretch this timing by keeping the solution in a dark place, such as a light-proof bag or light-proof chemical storage bottle. I have stored a solution like this for a year and used it successfully. It is always worth experimenting.

Coating the paper

Coating the chosen substrate (base layer) is quick and simple. This process does not need to be in a pitch-black room, just draw the curtains or cover the windows completely. With no direct sunlight coming into the room and falling onto your work surface, it is safe to coat the paper.

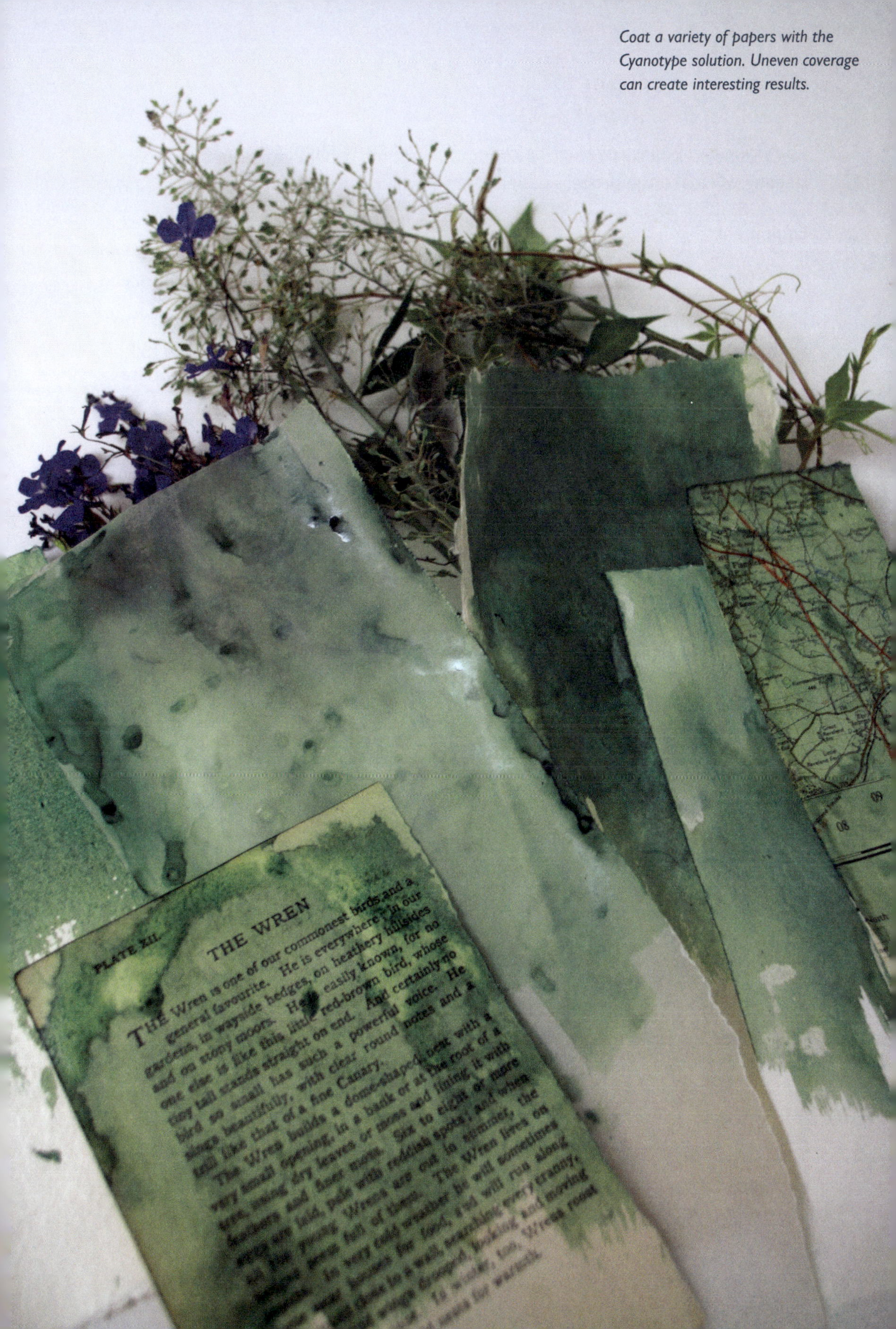

Coat a variety of papers with the Cyanotype solution. Uneven coverage can create interesting results.

PLATE XII.

THE WREN

THE Wren is one of our commonest birds and a general favourite. He is everywhere in our gardens, in wayside hedges, on heathery hillsides and on stony moors. He is easily known, for no one else is like this little red-brown bird, whose tiny tail stands straight on end. And certainly no bird so small has such a powerful voice. He sings beautifully, with clear round notes and a trill like that of a fine Canary.

The Wren builds a dome-shaped nest with a very small opening, in a bank or at the root of a tree, among dry leaves or moss and lining it with feathers and fine moss. Six to eight or more eggs, white, or white with reddish spots, are laid.

1   Cover the work surface with a plastic clothand wear rubber gloves – the solution will stain worktops and skin blue – and lay your chosen substrate on top.

2   Dip your foam applicator into the jar of mixed cyanotype chemicals and wipe it over the paper in an even coating. Your paper will turn a yellow-green colour. Do not saturate or pool the chemical on the surface.

Try coating different weights of paper – the only limitation is that it needs to withstand washing in water for a length of time. Try using old book paper, cotton rag paper and delicate tissue papers. The more delicate the paper, the more carefully it needs to be handled during the final rinsing.

Some papers are more absorbent than others and will use more of the chemical. Beware of papers where the chemical sits on the surface as this may just wash off after exposure and not produce a print.

3   Put the paper in a dark room to dry naturally, or dry carefully with a cool hairdryer.

4   When the sheets of coated paper are dry, place in a black, light-proof photographic bag. (Do not use a black bin bag as these are not light proof.) This bag of coated paper does not have to be used immediately; kept in a dark, dry place, the paper will be ready to use whenever you like. You can even take the bag on a walk and use the papers on location.

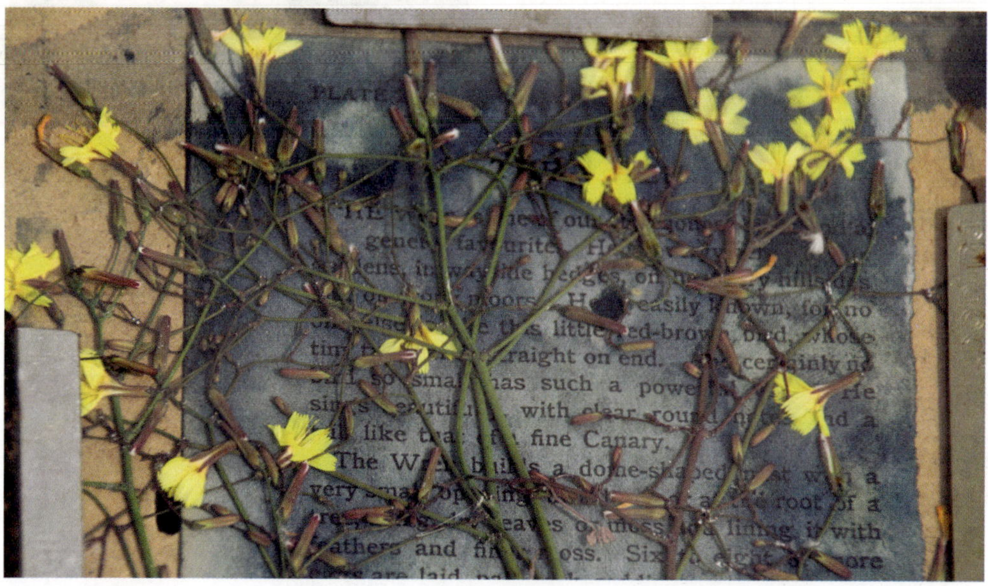

Delicate pressed vegetation will lead to delicate prints.

Exposing the paper

1   Remove the glass from the clip frame and have at least four bulldog clips to hand.

2   In a dull room protected from direct sunlight, take the coated cyanotype paper from its bag and lay it on the board of the clip frame. Arrange pressed or fresh flowers, leaves or grasses onto the surface of the paper.

Place the clean glass onto the composition and clamp the edges with bulldog clips to ensure tight contact between subject and paper. Be careful not to let the clips overlap the paper as this will leave rectangular white marks on the paper. Place in strong sunshine, ensuring the clip frame is facing the direction of the sun and that nothing is casting a shadow over the work. Once outside and exposed to the sun, the yellow-green paper will turn darker green. The optimum exposure should change the green to blue-grey and sometimes a bronze colour. The colour change is the best indication as to how everything is developing. Exposure times will vary depending on the cloud cover and time of day.

Choose a bright sunny summer day for the first experiments as the colour change in the paper will be quick and obvious.

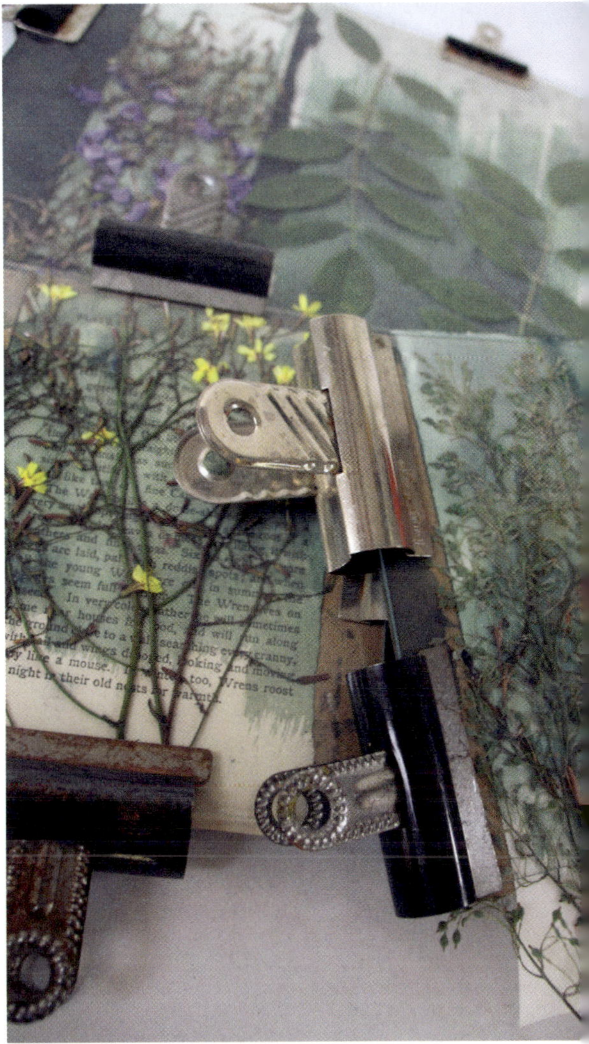

Clamp everything between boards and glass. Expose until the solution looks grey.

A longer exposure time will be needed if it's overcast, early or late in the day and during the winter months when the sun is lower in the sky. However, during midsummer excellent results can be achieved on a cloudy day.

3   When the sample has changed colour, take the clip frame into the shade. Release the clips and carefully take off the glass. Tip the leaves and flowers off the paper, then plunge the paper into a bucket of clean water and agitate. Rinse the paper for 5 to 10 minutes until the green-grey colour comes away and the white areas look clear. Do not rub the image as this will damage it. Rinse more than you think as any unexposed, unrinsed chemical will expose during drying and turn the whole print dark blue. Change the water in the bucket regularly between prints. The cyanotype chemical will wash away from the areas that were covered with the masking materials leaving white images. Unmasked areas will turn a deep blue.

4   Hang the finished print up to dry. The cyanotype blue will intensify as the print dries.

Take care when working in strong sunshine, protect bare skin with sunscreen and wear a hat.

Toning, not just blue

With practice and persistence, cyanotype printing is a very rewarding technique that captures the details and spirit of delicate flowers and the shapes of leaves and twigs. But this process does not always have to produce a blueprint.

Cyanotype prints can be changed from strong blue to a gentle yellow, then toned to faded brown. Try experimenting with differing strengths of solutions of coffee, black and green tea or even red wine using the following method:

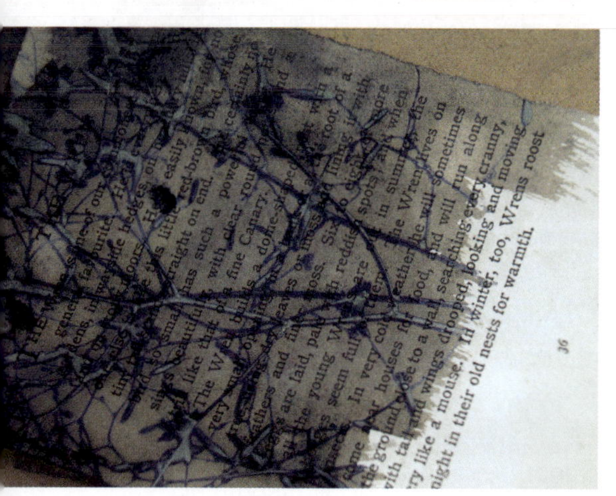

Unclamp the print when ready. The print will look exciting, but it will change completely. Take a photo of this stage.

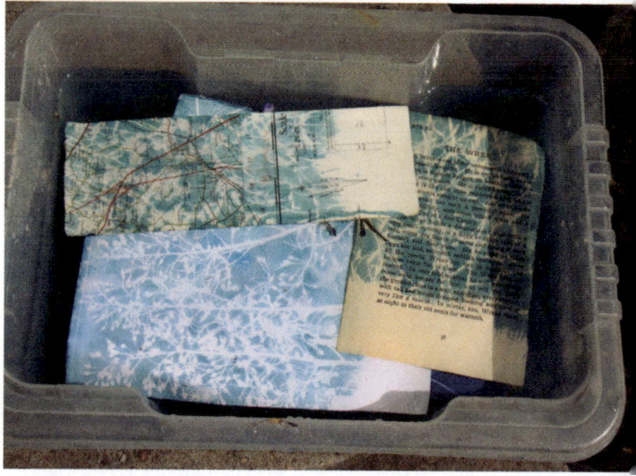

Rinse exposed prints and agitate gently. Rinse for longer than expected.

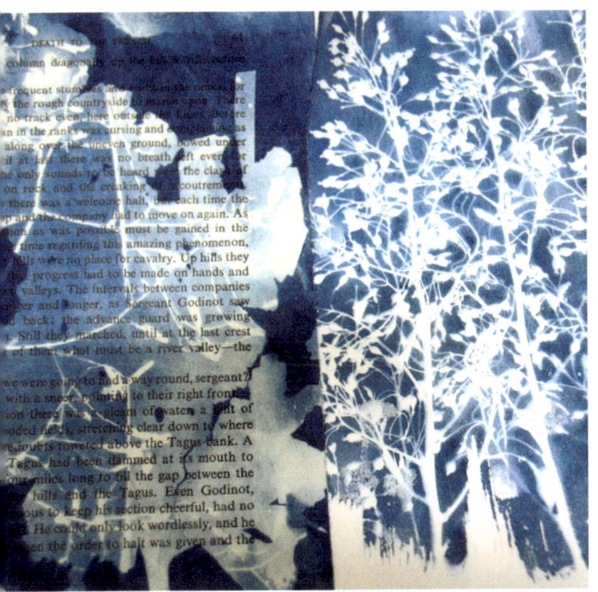

Double exposures work well. Recoat a delicate print and expose with a large specimen.

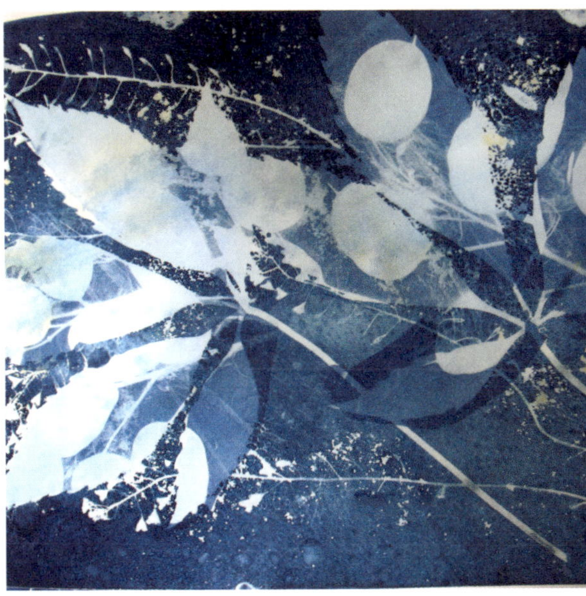

Printed samples, the larger the leaf stencil the more solid looking the print.

1   Dissolve 1–2 teaspoons of soda ash into a litre of warm water. This can be done in a screw topped bottle and stored for later use.

2   Pour the soda ash mixture into a tray and lay the dry, blue cyanotype in the tray of liquid. Watch carefully as the blue starts to fade into a pale yellow. Remove the print when the desired yellow tone is reached – if left too long, the print can be bleached until it becomes indistinct. If that happens the image can be restored using the following instructions:

    i.   Brew a very strong pot of tea or coffee and pour into a tray. You can also use red wine.

    ii. Wearing gloves, remove the print from the soda ash solution, rinse in fresh water and transfer it into your tray of strong brewed tea, coffee or red wine. Soak for 10–15 minutes, or until the required tone is achieved. The image will return but will be brown or brownish-red instead of blue. The tannin in the brewed mixtures stain the bleached areas giving the images a vintage look.

You might also like to try the tea, coffee or red wine baths with blue, unbleached cyanotypes and compare the different results in the toned colour.

Examples of waxing prints and toning double and treble exposed prints.

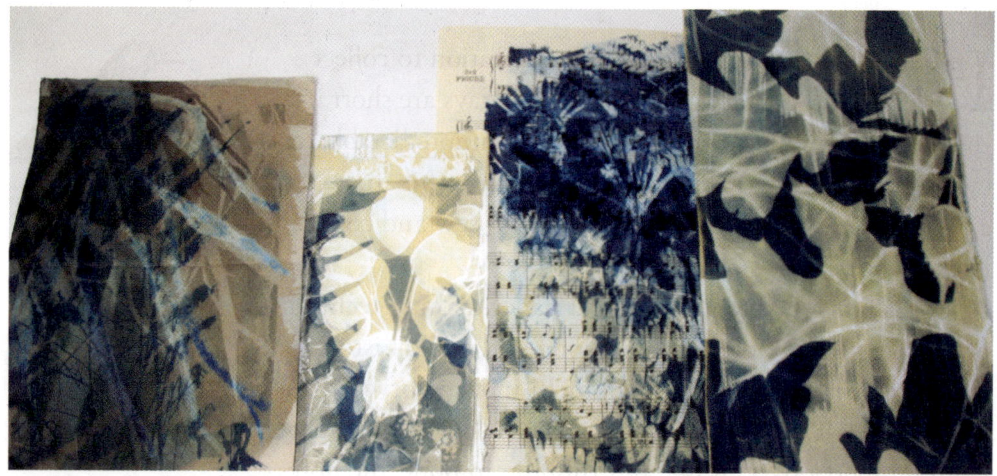

Extending the toning process

An exciting extension of this process is to take a white candle and draw lines onto the dry, blue cyanotype. The wax will resist the bleaching of the soda ash leaving blue areas in the yellow. After bleaching, dry the print and draw with the wax again. Soaked in tea, or other chosen toner, the wax will hold the yellow and blue in the print, while unwaxed areas will tone brown. Suddenly cyanotype prints are multi-coloured and not just blue or toned brown – this will add further creative possibilities to explore from a simple photographic technique.

Cyanotype is a process that lends itself to experimentation, so enjoy playing. You might like to try partially covering paper with the chemicals.

- Dry the print, recoat with the cyanotype solution and expose again with more plant material. This will build up a complex layered image of different shades of blue. When this image is toned, different layers and colours will emerge (see image above).

- Place three-dimensional objects onto the surface and see what image is produced as a result.

- Have prints partially dipped into toning trays.

With a bottle of cyanotype mixture prepared, or a few coated papers in a black bag, it is possible to come back from a walk on a sunny day with leaves and grasses, or return from the allotment or garden with carrot tops and flowers at their peak, and record them in a cyanotype print. With a little ingenuity, this process can be made portable too so you can make cyanotypes out on location. Well worth exploring.

JOOMCHI

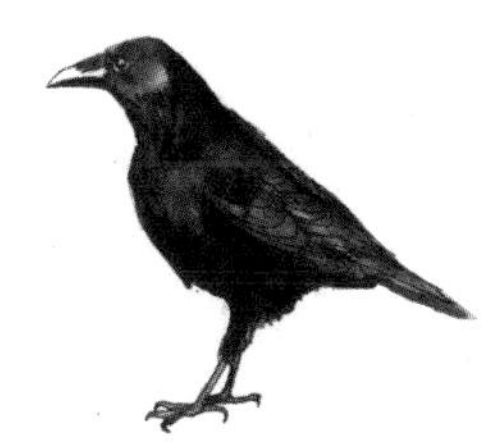

In the winter months there is little vegetation to collect for botanical contact printing and the days are short in the United Kingdom, making light levels unpredictable for cyanotype printing. Rather than let creativity hibernate, this is a good time to make felted paper to print, sew and collage with later in the year.

Joomchi is a 500-year-old felted paper-making technique originating from Korea. It has a long and noble history, with the Koreans actively making joomchi in the Goryeo Dynasty (918–1392). It is a simple process using long-fibred paper made from mulberry bark, water and rubbing to bond the fibres together. The more layers there are and the longer the papers are worked, the tougher and more textile-like it becomes. Joomchi can be treated like cloth that can be stitched, printed and collaged and is often sewn into clothing.

The right papers

Mulberry (Kozo) paper has long fibres that, with energetic massaging and squeezing, tangle and adhere firmly creating a strong textile-style substrate. This makes it ideal for joomchi (and it is readily available from paper suppliers and specialist art stores), but you can also use a variety of other handmade papers. It is worth experimenting with whatever is to hand as it often surprising how well an experimental paper will felt together.

Collecting papers can be compelling and not too expensive as a sheet or two will produce several surfaces to work with. Try Japanese washi (washi literally means Japanese paper) mitsumata, gampi, Indian cotton rag papers (commonly known as khadi paper and available in a variety of surfaces and colours), Tibetan tissue and lokta paper.

Avoid papers with waxed or plastic coatings as this will make them moisture resistant and not suitable for the wet

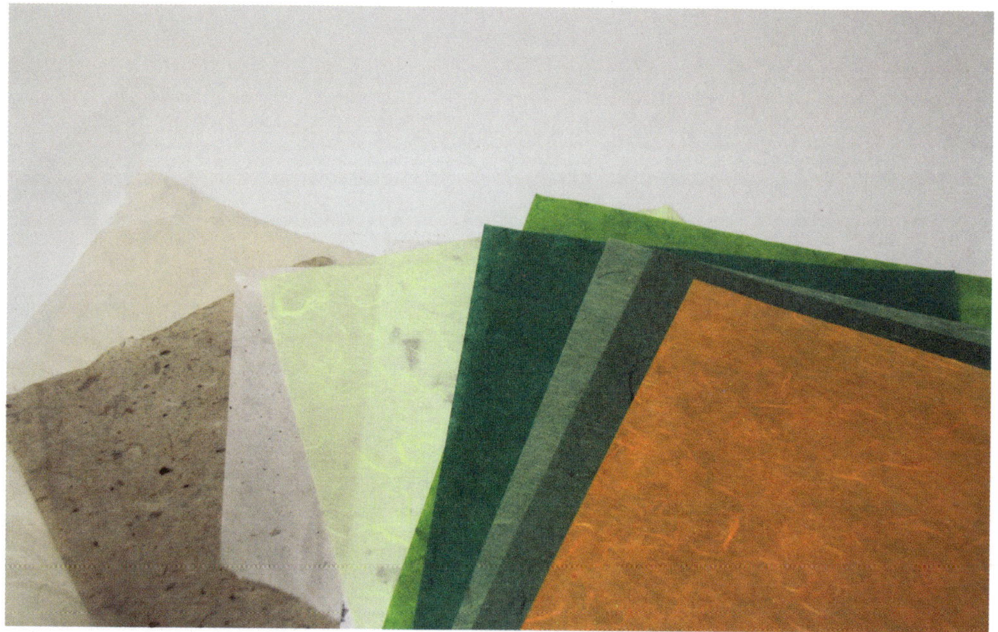

Plain and coloured handmade papers.

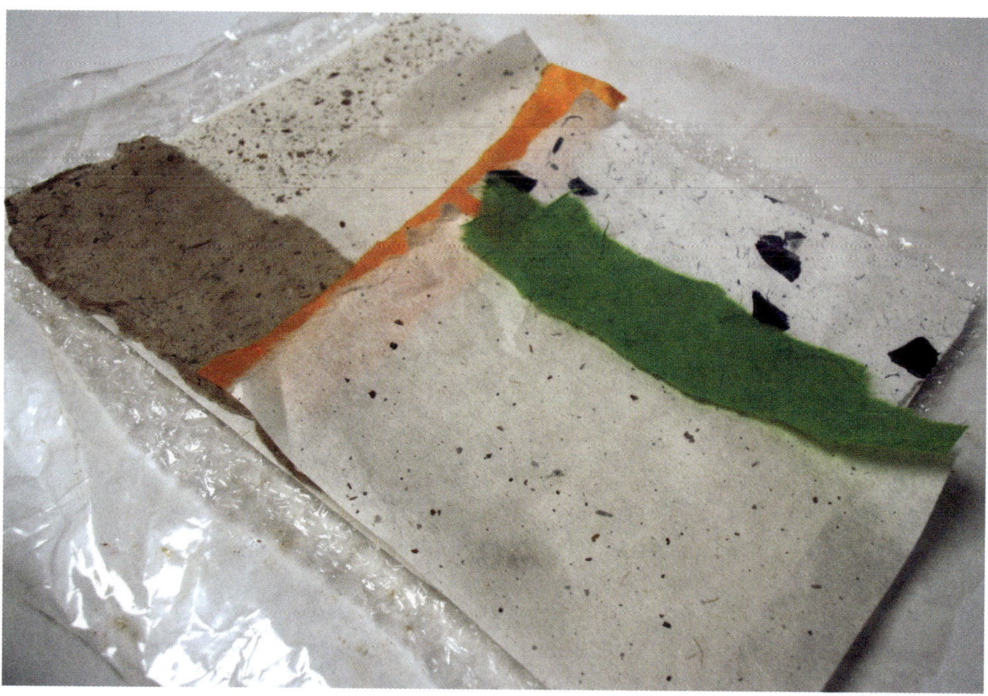

Layered papers onto a plain sheet base. Adding flashes of strong colour.

felting process. Be aware too that some commercially pre-dyed papers will bleed colour which will affect the outcome. This may cause a pleasing effect, however some colours, particularly reds, can dominate other neutral tones. Some handmade papers with petals and grasses embedded into the surface may not felt with the surfaces of other papers.

Depending on what papers have been used, try using the botanical contact and cyanotype prints made earlier in the year. If these surfaces stood up to the boiling and rinsing used in both printmaking techniques, adding them to the layers used to create joomchi should not be too much of a problem. Using printed papers in this way adds a personal touch to the work.

A natural composition of handmade papers.

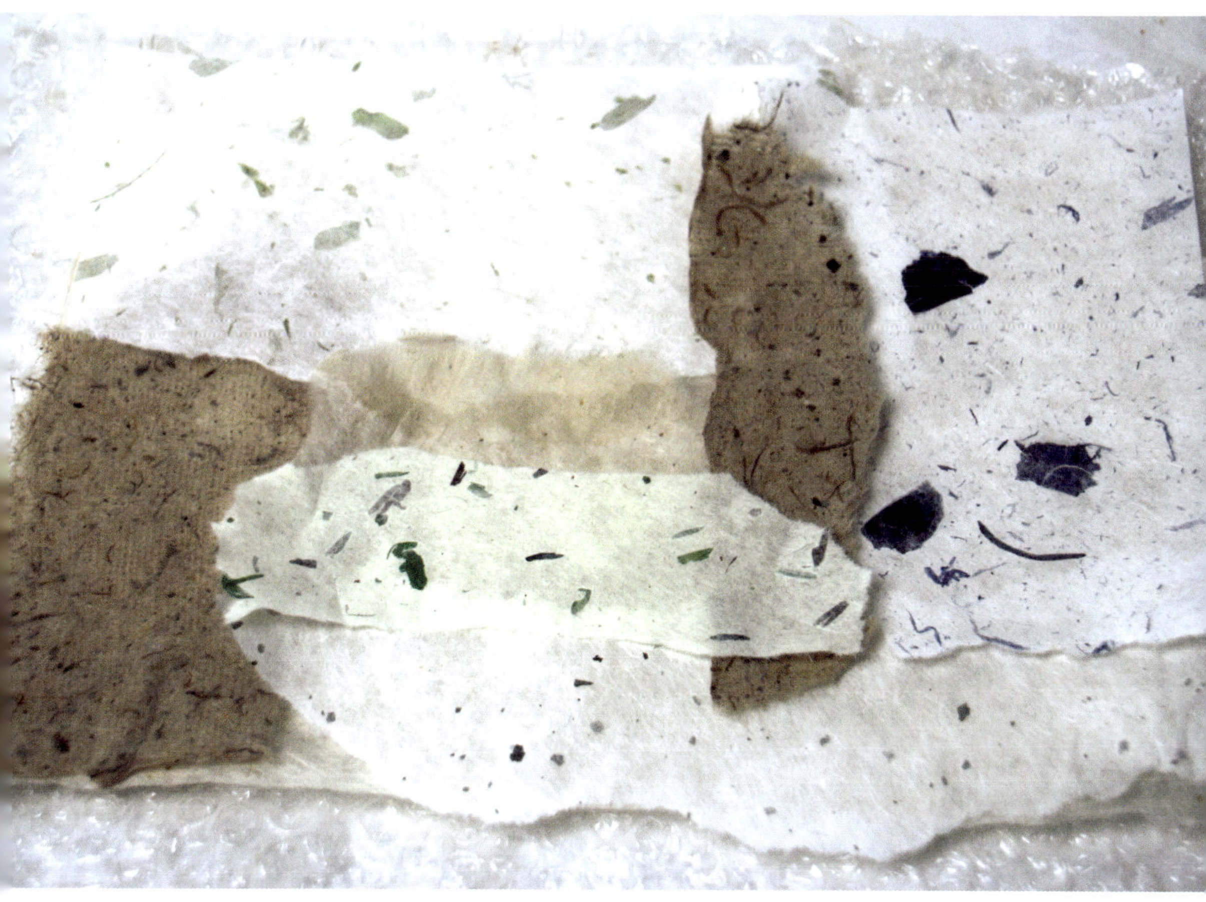

Equipment

- Spray bottle filled with water
- A sheet of plastic to cover the work surface
- 2 x sheets of bubble wrap, slightly larger than the sheet of joomchi to be made

Materials

- A variety of long fibred papers such as mulberry, khadi, Tibetan tissue, kozo, mitsumata and gampi (A couple of sheets of one type of paper in contrasting colours will suffice but the more variety there is, the more interesting the finished sample will be.)
- Try wet-strength tissue, newsprint, old book papers
- Printed newsprint, tissue and khadi paper marked using techniques earlier or from other chapters
- PVA glue (If there are papers that do not bond during the felting process, or a hole appears, glue is useful for small repairs when the piece is dry.)

Gathering everything together before starting will make the process easier

The felting processes

1 Cover the worksurface with a piece of plastic larger than the joomchi to be made. It is a very wet process so covering the worksurface will help contain excess moisture.

2 Lay down one piece of bubble wrap larger than the desired sheet of finished joomchi and place a complete sheet of neutral-coloured mulberry, or other long-fibred paper, on top. Start with an A4 sheet. Larger pieces can be attempted when the technique is perfected. Spray the surface with water. The paper should be completely wet.

3 Add torn or cut pieces of other papers in layers. Ensure that the surface of the supporting paper is totally covered and that the sections of the added papers overlap. Cover the base paper with two to three larger pieces to begin with. Stay within the boundary of the base sheet. Spray the surface with water again, wetting all the papers evenly and completely.

4 Repeat step 3 until the surface is patchworked with a variety of textures and colours. Smaller pieces can now be added, ensuring everything overlaps and holes are not made – unless holes are desired. Spray each new layer with water so that the surface is wet. This will help to bond the fibres together later in the process.

5 Check that there is even coverage and add small pieces of paper to any thin areas or places where holes could develop. This will add to the texture and patchwork appearance of the finished piece.

Note: For the first few sheets, cover the surface with at least two complete layers. The resulting joomchi will be easier to handle. When the technique is perfected thinner papers and pieces with deliberate holes can be made.

6   Give the surface one last even spray of water, then cover the wet surface completely with the second piece of bubble wrap, slightly larger than the finished piece. You will have a bubble wrap sandwich with a wet paper filling.

7   Starting at the top, pick up both edges of the bubble wrap and start to roll up the 'sandwich' of bubble wrap and wet paper. Roll as tightly as possible. Holding firmly between both hands, squeeze and roll. Fold the roll in half, squeeze and rub together.

8   Carefully unroll the sandwich and turn it round and re-roll. Fold the roll in half again, then massage it between your hands and squeeze.

9   Wipe the resulting water from the worksurface then unroll the sandwich, carefully ease off the top piece of bubble wrap and gently smooth the wet paper flat. Respray with water. If the fibres look as if they are attaching to each other, move on to step 11. However, if the surface still looks loose and unbonded, reroll into the bubble wrap the other way and hand roll again.

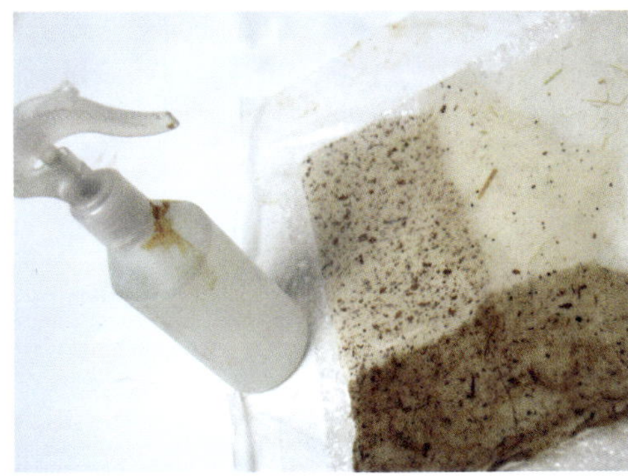

Soak everything with water using a spray bottle

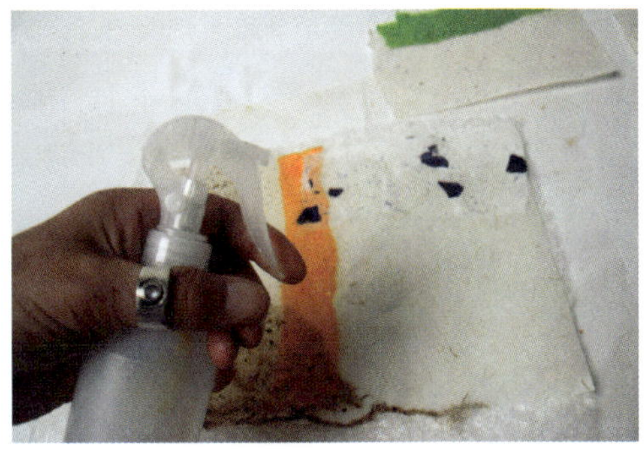

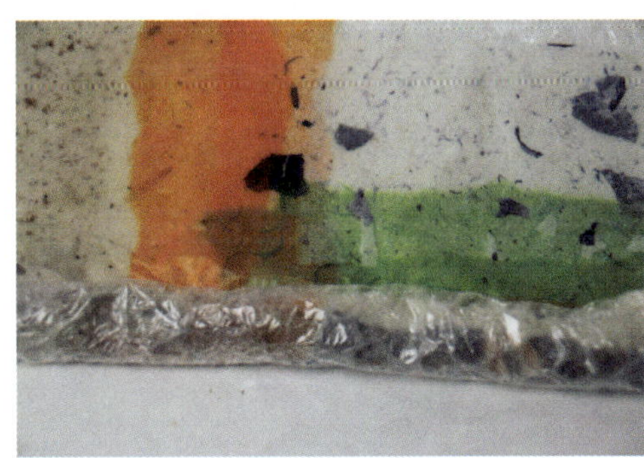

Pick up edges and roll with the bubble wrap

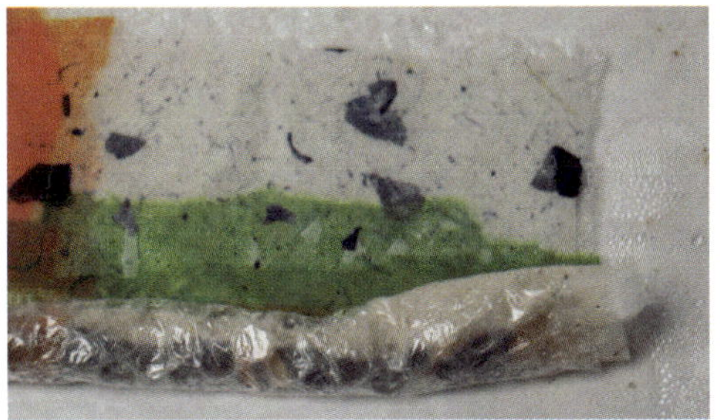

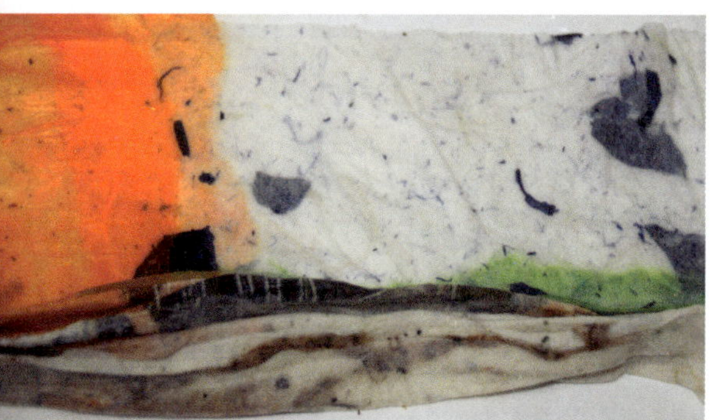

After pre-felting in the bubble wrap, pleat the paper together. It should be wet.

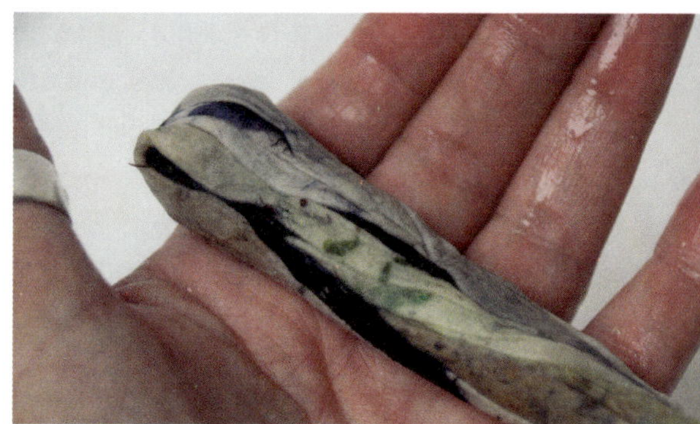

Fold the pleat in half and roll and squeeze with both hands.

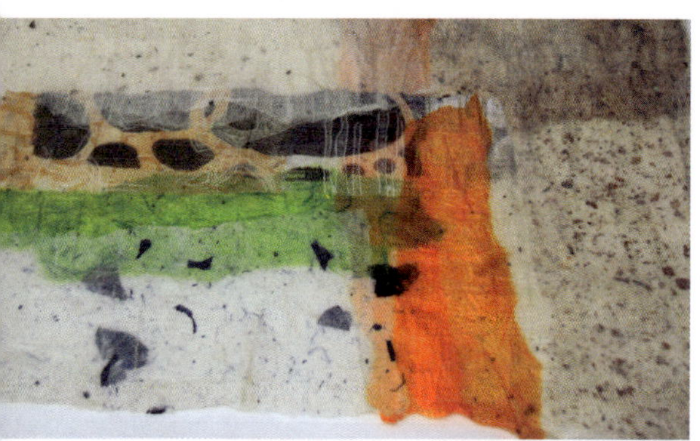

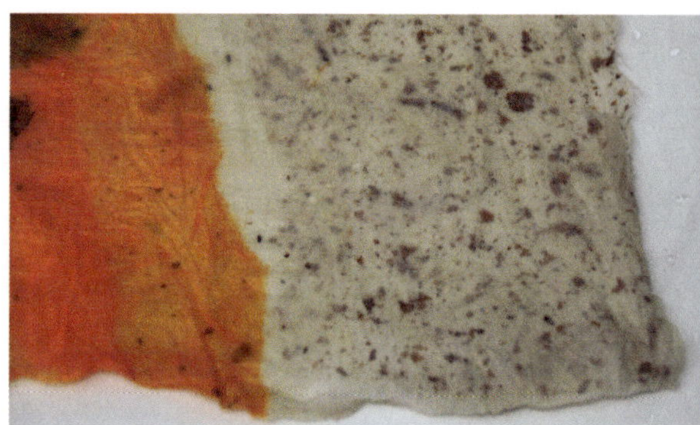

After pleating and squeezing, gently ease the pleats apart to see if the paper fibres have bonded.

10 The fibres of the paper should have started to bond together. If a hole has appeared, you can reinforce the area with another piece of paper. Spray everything again with water and reroll the sandwich again between the hands. It is the water and agitation that felts the paper fibres together. When you are satisfied that the paper is bonded, ease the joomchi off both pieces of bubble wrap and start to manipulate the piece by hand.

11 Starting from the bottom, pleat the paper using your fingertips to create a length of pleated paper. Fold the pleat in half and squeeze together, ensuring that the work is wet. Form into a ball and squeeze firmly in your hands. Unfold the piece gently, easing the paper apart. If you have used long-fibred papers, this piece will stay together. If you have incorporated experimental papers, which have not adhered, simply remove them and set aside to glue on later.

12 Continue to pleat, wet and squeeze until the joomchi has bonded together as required. The resulting piece of paper will have shrunk as the fibres cling together and it may be asymmetric in shape. Some of the papers will look translucent when wet, but these may become opaque on drying.

13 Hang out the joomchi and allow it to dry completely. When dry, glue or stitch any wayward pieces that are resisting the felting process.

Please note that once the sheet is dry it cannot be re-felted as the felting process sets the fibres after being worked and agitated.

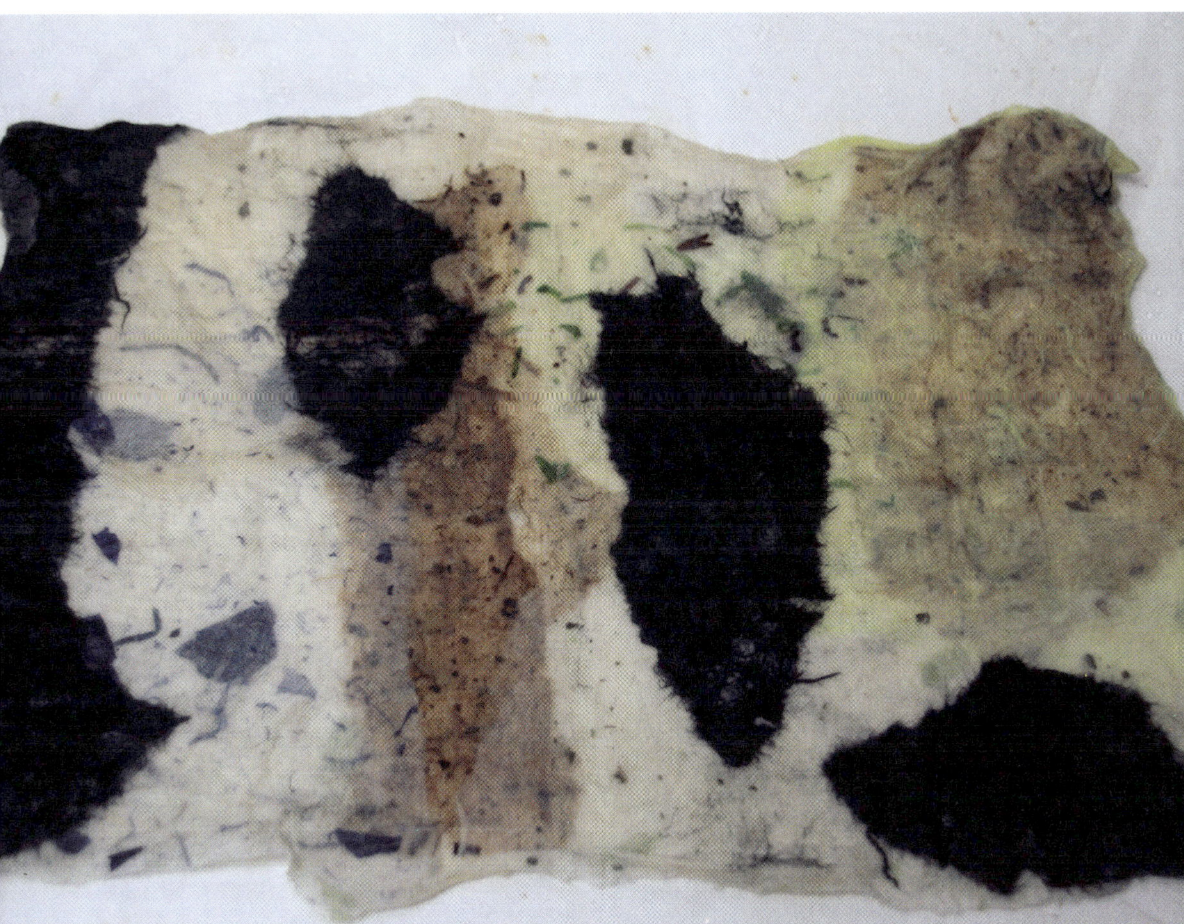

The fibres will bond at the edges and the piece will shrink. Ease out the paper and stretch slightly.

When dry the paper will strengthen and
become opaque.

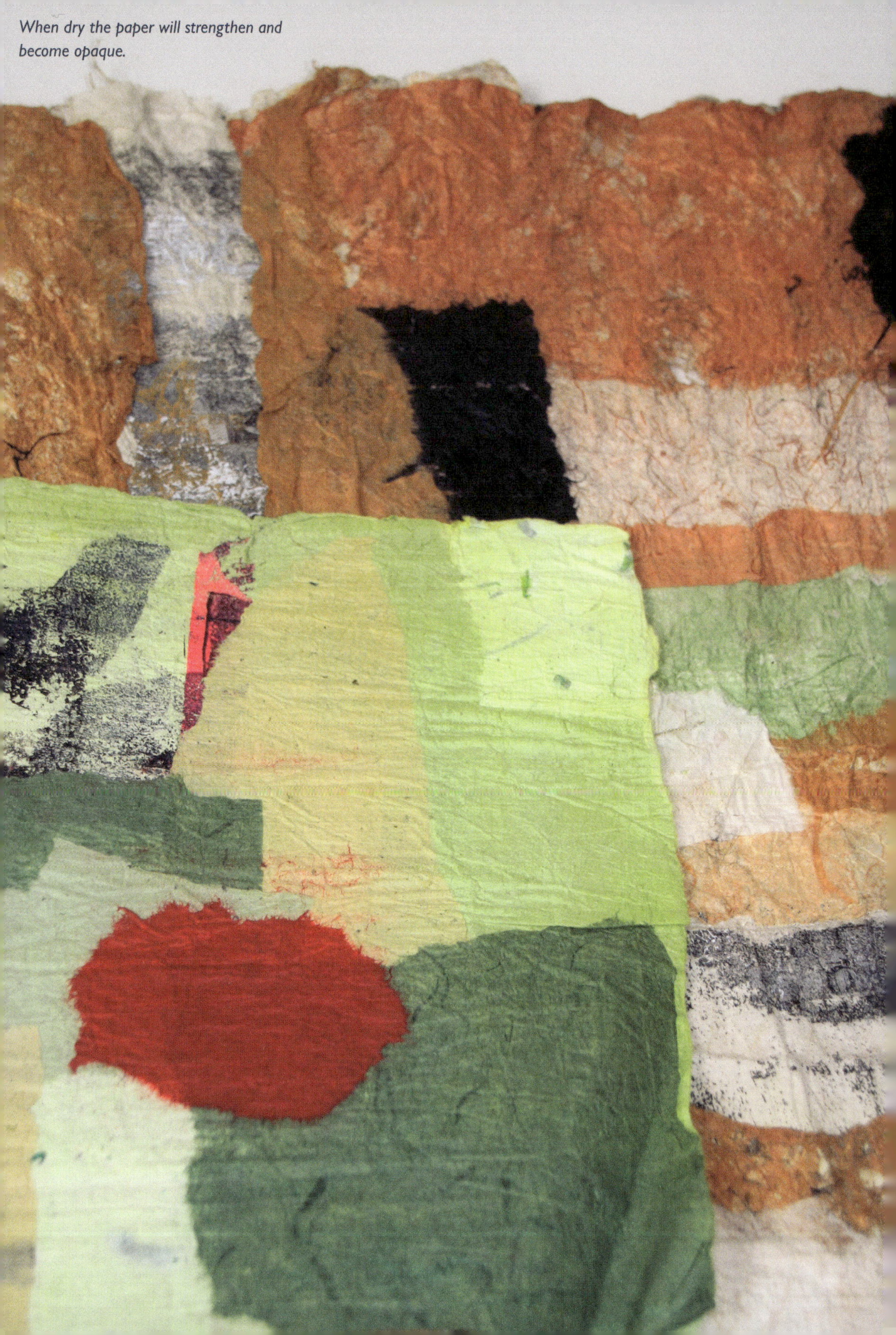

Creative extensions

Once this technique is mastered using long-fibred papers that will felt together with ease, it can be rewarding to experiment with papers that look as if they will not bond. Look at that collection of old books, newspapers and manuscripts. Vintage papers were often made from rag. (Paper made before the mid-nineteenth century was largely composed of rag fibres.) However, with practise it is possible to layer and attach paper to the surface using another felted piece to hold it in place. Some papers will work well, others may partially attach to the surface leaving loose edges but it's nothing that cannot be mended with a bit of glue or stitching here and there.

Joomchi creates a durable robust surface but will not stand up to the boiling and rinsing processes used in botanical contact and cyanotype printing. It's best to experiment with these two processes using unusual handmade papers first, then try felting the resulting printed papers together.

Joomchi adds a new slant to collage as different colours and patterns of papers become integrated to create a single surface that is attractive, sturdy and can be folded, stitched and glued.

Coating the surface with clear acrylic mediums or wax will brighten the colours and add to its moisture resistance. Most papers will dry leaving solid opaque

colours that will obscure the layers underneath so pre-planning which papers are in the final layer will help you achieve the desired effect.

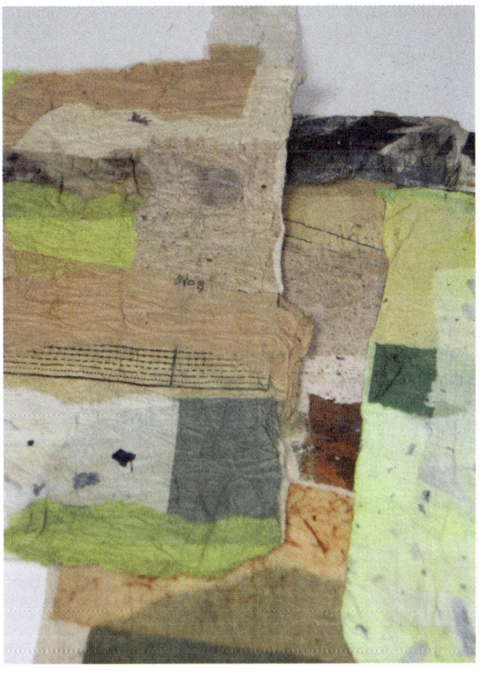

Dressmaking tissue and printed tissues can be included. Just add a bit of glue to anything that will not bond with the felting process.

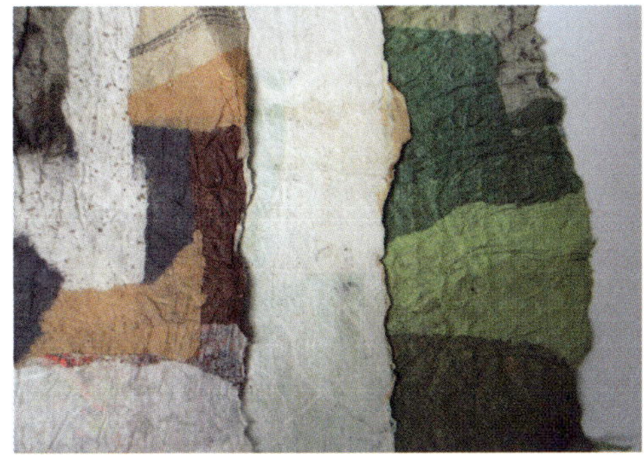

Comparing the back and front of sheets of joomchi. Sometimes the sheet will retain the bubble wrap impression.

DEVELOPING COMBINATIONS

Botanical contact printing, cyanotype images and joomchi are very different techniques. Each process can produce a completed piece but, once you are confident with the process, the next creative step is to experiment with combinations and create different outcomes by blending two or more techniques together.Experiment, explore and create different outcomes by blending two or more techniques together.

A composition using joomchi, botanical contact printing, monoprinted flowers and leaves. Fresh leaves have been stitched in place.

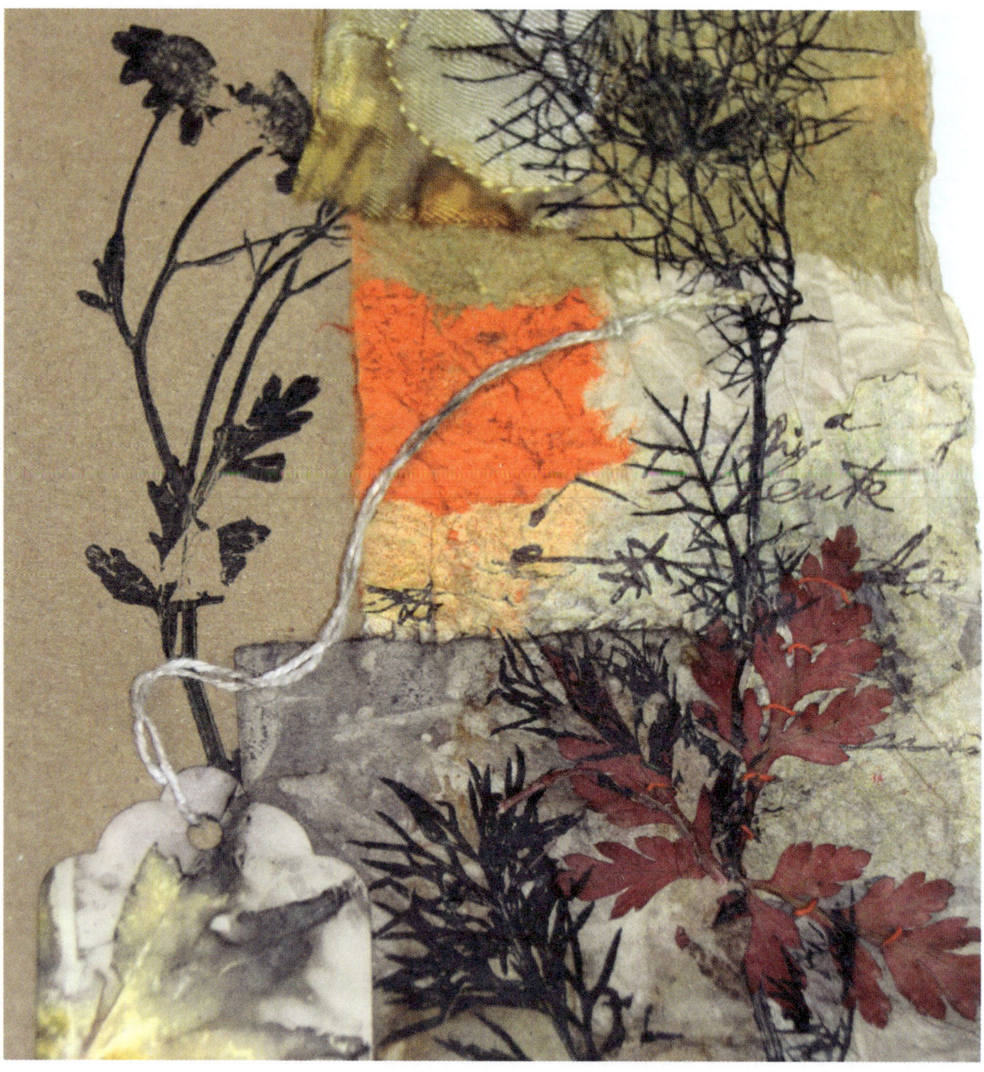

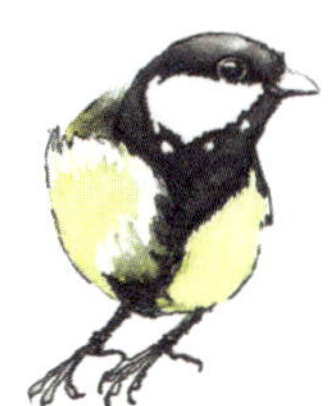

Here are a few combinations to try:

- When collecting leaves and flowers to boil in a bundle, keep a few back and press between kitchen paper in a heavy book to use later. Then use the lightly pressed leaves as a mask in a cyanotype print on the next sunny day, or to monoprint with during the autumn and winter. This uses a collection in several different ways.

- Take a cyanotype image and partially layer with wire wool, onion skin and leaves, bundle and boil as instructed earlier (p34–37). Combining cyanotype with botanical contact printing will produce some interesting effects. The chemicals in the bundle will change the blue of the cyanotype, producing new colours.

- Use a dry botanical contact print and partially paint it with cyanotype chemicals. Mask out areas with leaves and flowers and expose them to the sun. The chemicals will react with the botanical print, changing the nature of the blueprint.

- Experiment with long-fibre papers when you are botanical and cyanotype printing in spring and summer, then store these papers for felting into a sheet of joomchi in the autumn and winter. This will connect seasonal activities creating personalised sheets that hold the narrative of collecting throughout the year.

COLLECT, PRINT, EXPERIMENT

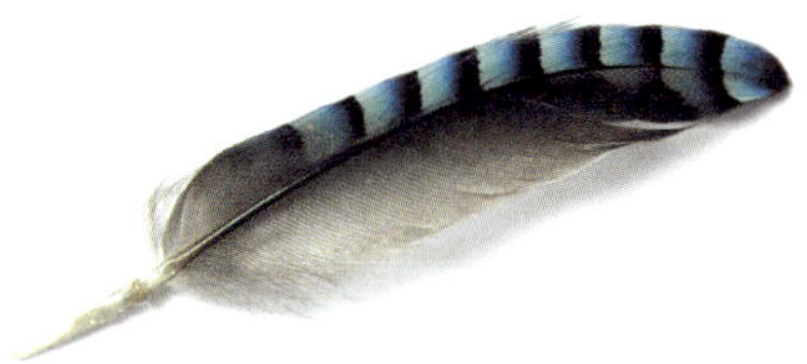

THINKING IN MATTER

LOUISE RICHARDSON

Louise Richardson is a multidisciplinary artist specialising in mixed media sculpture, textiles and photography. Her practice involves exploring ideas of memory and identity, refining and collecting ideas and materials to create a resource library for new artworks.

Richardson has exhibited nationally and internationally and her works are included in various private and public collections. She lives and works in Norwich, United Kingdom.

My work unfolds slowly, through accumulative, repetitive gestures that measure duration and attention. Slowness is a way of seeing, a method of dwelling in the present. The studio becomes a space where making and noticing coincide; a place where each mark is both an act and an observation, transforming ordinary materials and revealing subtle connections between people, moments and time.

Nature is not an external subject but one that enters the work directly or indirectly. I try not to impose form so much as negotiate with what these materials already know how to do. Colours alter, fibres shift and tighten as air dries them. Rather than resisting these processes, I work with them. I think of the pieces as a conversation between human intention and materiality – an act of coexistence.

Materials carry memory. Each is an archive of relations. When I assemble them, I am not inventing so much as tracing lines of connection – between object and origin, between craft and ecology, between the living and the remembered. The work becomes a form of material thinking, where knowledge resides in texture and contact as much as in an idea.

My language of making combines found and processed materials, often influenced by domestic craft, stitching, mending and layering. These are gestures historically tied to maintenance and repair – often unrecorded, but continuous across generations. To work within that lineage is to acknowledge the quiet perseverance of those who came before: objects made not for display but for use and, in doing so, sustained material culture itself. In my practice, these gestures return as inheritance, reflection and acknowledgement – a way of linking personal making to collective history and storytelling.

Lead: found feathers, mixed media.

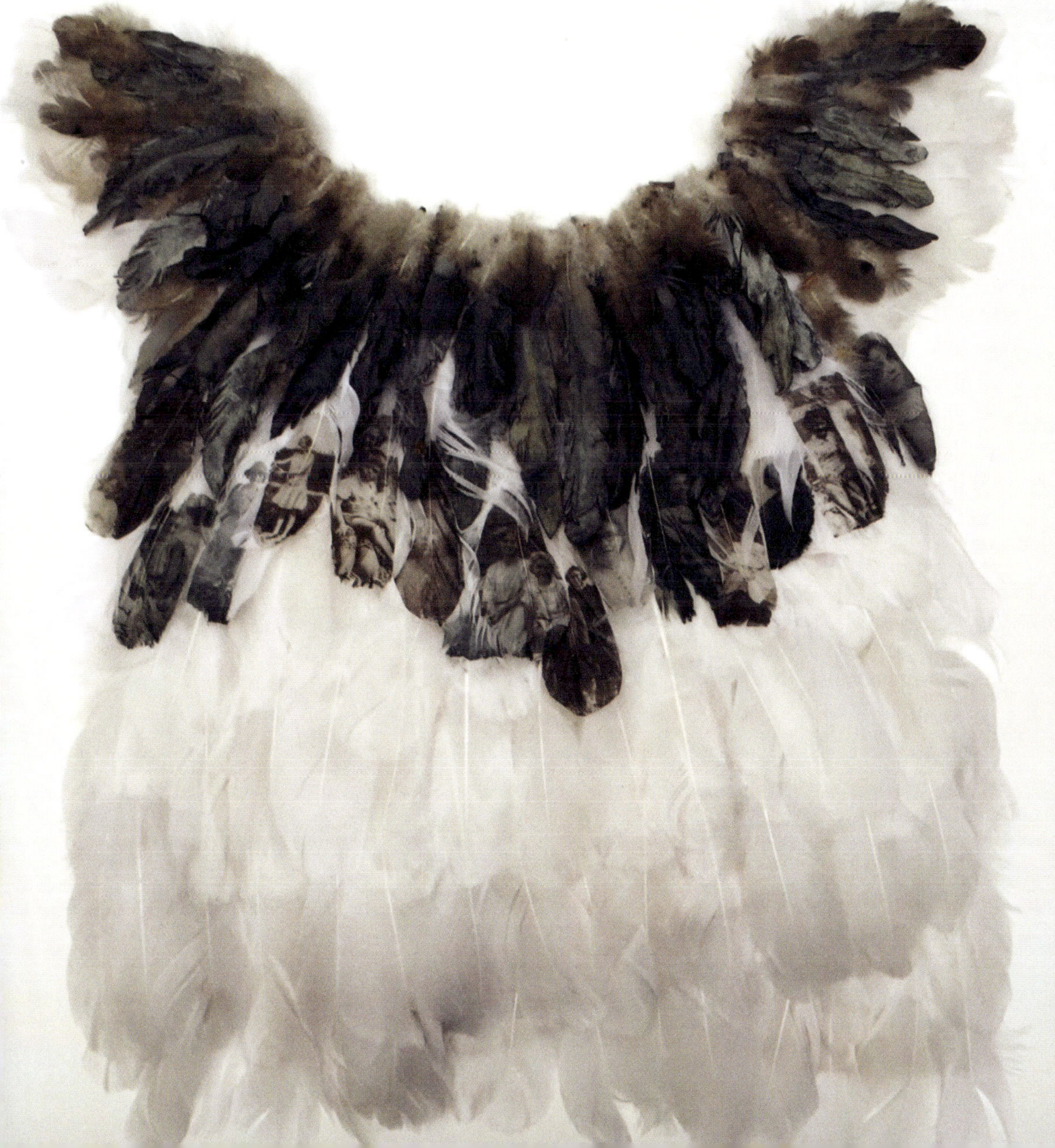

The work connects me to a longer history – largely domestic and female, often unknown. Its knowledge is transmitted through gesture rather than language: how to hold a needle, how to tension thread, how to judge the weight of cloth. These actions are inherited forms of thought, specific yet widely shared. When I repeat them, I feel a continuity that is both cultural and personal. It is through these gestures that memory becomes tangible, and through repetition that it becomes visible.

Many of the pieces I make are functionally impossible and made from transient materials. This releases them from the logic of consumption and allows them to exist as objects of reflection. Through their arrested function, they ask what it means to value something for the care invested in it, rather than its efficiency. Materials continue to shift; to preserve the un-preservable is not a contradiction but an acknowledgement of matter's continuity. Fabric that fades, thread that loosens – these are not faults, but evidence of life. The work participates in time rather than resisting it.

Working by hand is also a form of research. Process reveals what theory can only suggest – how structure depends on fragility, how attention alters perception, how time behaves when measured through touch. The studio functions as both laboratory and refuge; a space where material and thought evolve together.

The intimacy of making keeps the scale of the work human. The size of the pieces invites closeness rather than distance. To encounter them is to sense the labour embedded in their surfaces – the hours, repetitions and adjustments that shaped them. That intimacy is not sentimental, but structural; it is how meaning enters the work.

I am often asked about narrative but the stories that arise are implied through the transformation of objects and the alchemy of materials. The process of making is fundamental; the time it takes to make transcends the piece and encourages the viewer to also take time – to observe and make connections with the work. The viewer's gaze is held, they are involved and included in the dialogue leading them to question the maker's intention and consider how one would feel owning or wearing this garment. All this aims to encourage storytelling and engagement with the piece, creating space for reflection and for seeing connections between material and environment. In this sense, slowness is both method and message: a declaration that attention itself is a creative act.

Razor shells, mixed media.

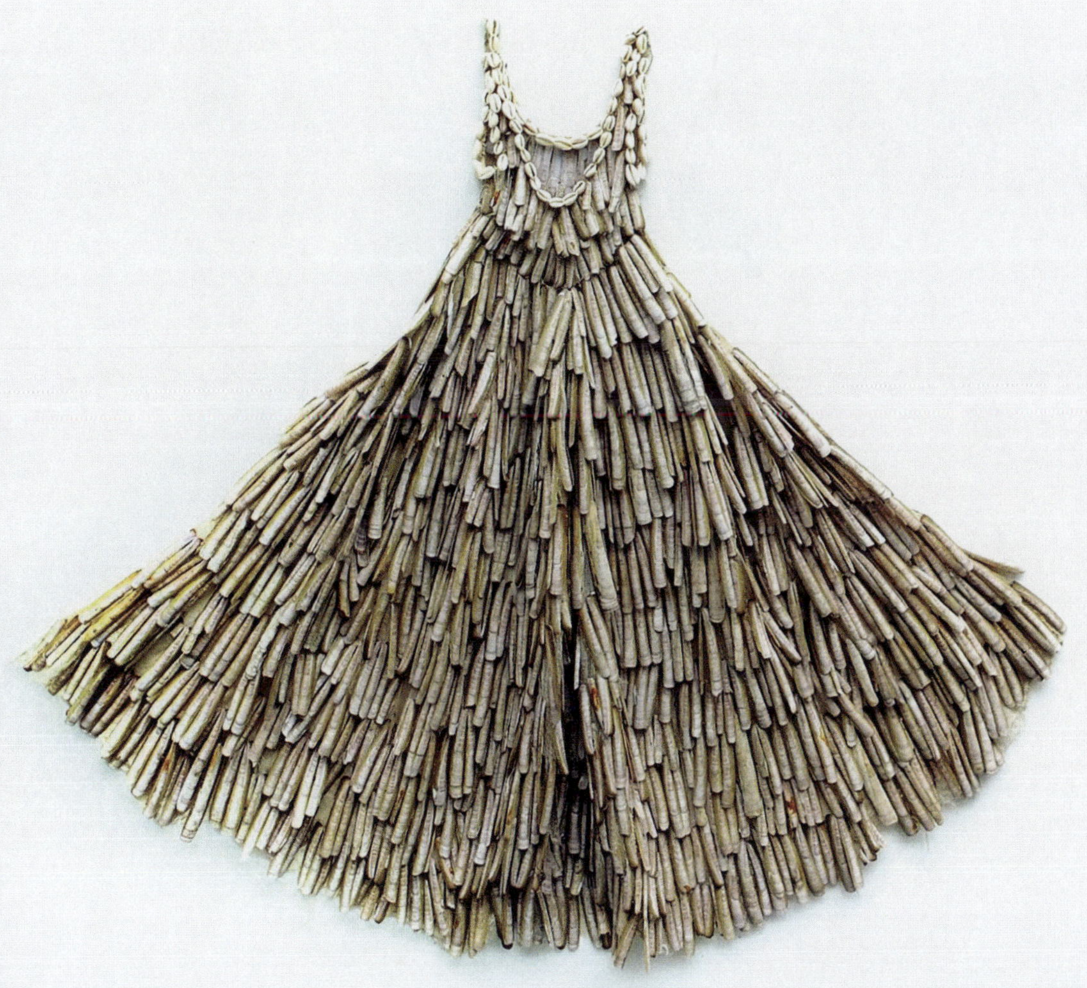

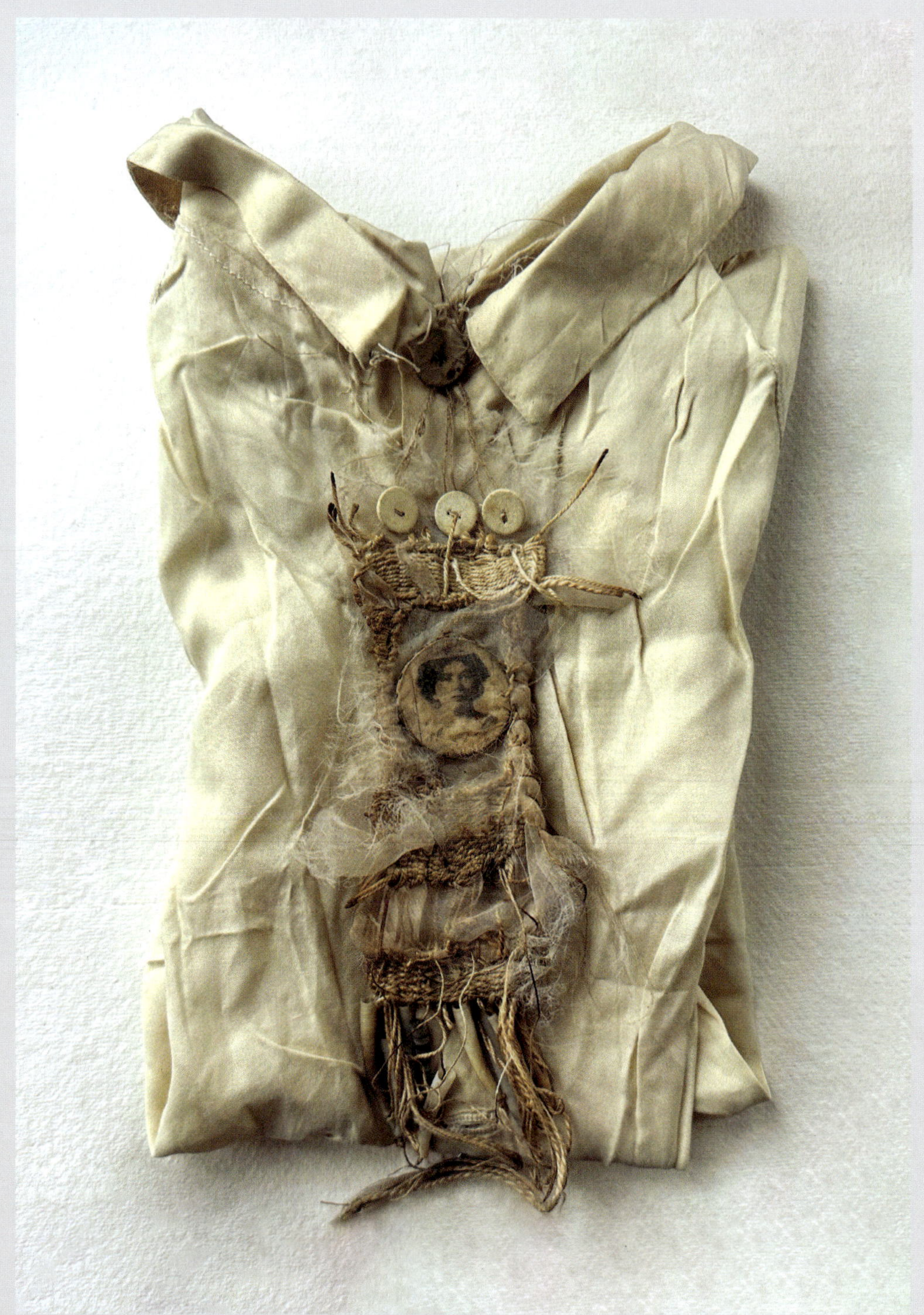

Sailor's Valentine, 2021

The natural world mirrors this rhythm. These shifts remind me that material and environment are inseparable. Even indoors, the work continues to breathe, absorb and respond. Making becomes a dialogue with impermanence; a way to inhabit rather than arrest transformation. The works have a quiet presence, but quietness is not absence; it is a way of creating space for observation, an equilibrium between care and letting go.

If there is repair in the work, it lies less in what is mended than in the recognition that repair is possible. To attend to what is fragile, to work with what is overlooked, is to affirm continuity even in the face of loss. Each fragment carries potential for re-combination, each material a record of previous lives. In assembling them, I do not erase their pasts, but allow those pasts to intersect. The resulting objects hold multiple moments at once: the now of their making, the then of their materials and the future of their inevitable change.

Ultimately, what I make is a form of thinking in matter. Through the slow intelligence of materials, I come to understand the relationship between human and environment, between history and present, between what is touched and what touches back. The work is not a statement but an exploration – through cloth, thread, natural objects and storytelling.

To make is to participate in a story larger than one's own, to add a small trace to a longer pattern of care. The finished pieces may eventually fade but the act of making – the attention it demands, the relations it reveals – continues. In that sense, the work is both record and offering: an acknowledgement of the materials that sustain us and of the histories, visible and invisible, that they carry forward.

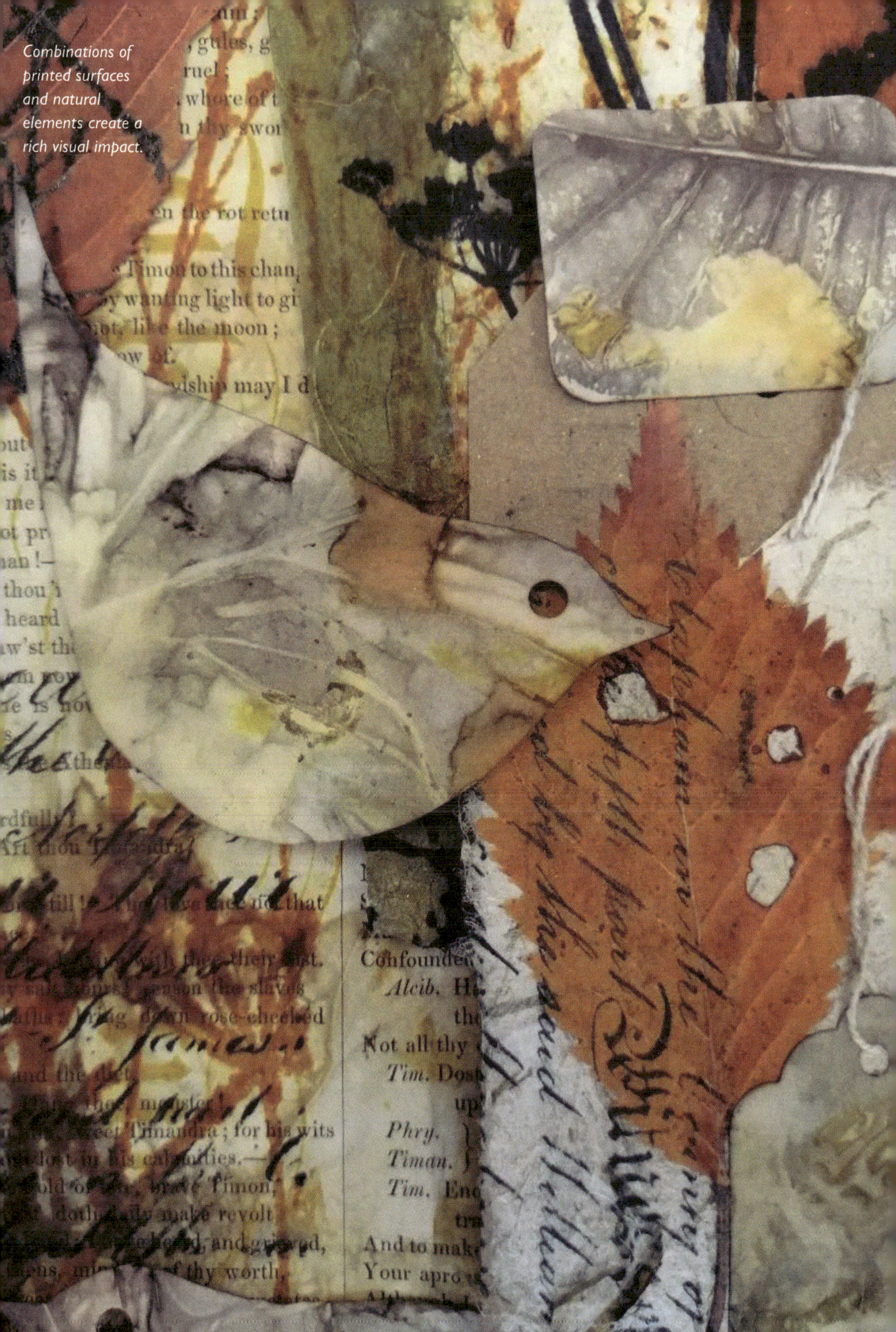

Combinations of
printed surfaces
and natural
elements create a
rich visual impact.

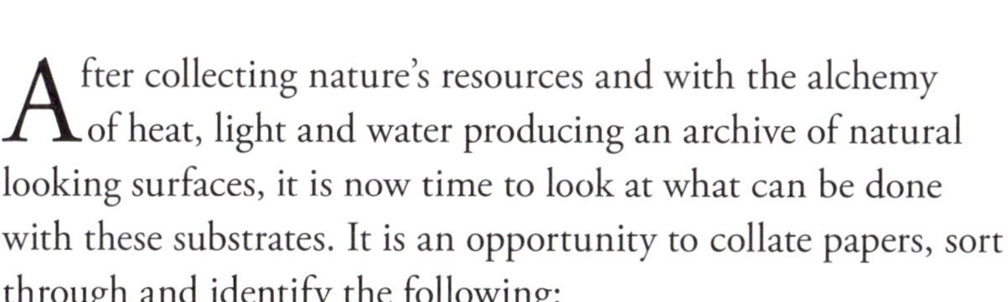

2

NATURAL COMPOSITIONS

After collecting nature's resources and with the alchemy of heat, light and water producing an archive of natural looking surfaces, it is now time to look at what can be done with these substrates. It is an opportunity to collate papers, sort through and identify the following:

- Prints that are too beautiful to touch or add to

- What has potential for further work

- Put aside pieces that have been less successful

Try not to throw anything away at this stage; surfaces that are vague, too strong or simply compare less favourably with others can all be kept for experimenting on before moving on to a treasured piece with confidence. Often, the less successful something is, the more it lends itself to experimentation. After all, there is nothing to lose and, by working on it, you may even turn its fortunes around.

These curated piles can then be clearly labelled 'keep', 'develop' or 'experiment' and stored ready for use. Of course, none of this is set in stone; labels will change and sheets of paper will move from one pile to another as pieces are developed and more natural resources are collected. Such is the nature of the creative process.

FURTHER COLLECTING

After the initial flurry of making surfaces, I often find my store of natural raw materials depleted, giving me the perfect excuse to go out foraging in the fresh air once again.

Collecting for natural compositions is about properly noticing what is in the environment; it is a careful, nuanced and mindful process. Once, coming back from my regular walk to a local park, I found a jay's feather on the verge. I wasn't looking for a jay's feather, but I noticed the crocuses growing in the grass and as I was very relaxed and aware of my surroundings, this jewel-coloured treasure caught my eye. It is now waiting to be incorporated into a natural composition. Collecting is about taking notice of the small things and calming a busy mind.

Making natural compositions on labels with botanical contact printing, including my precious jay feather.

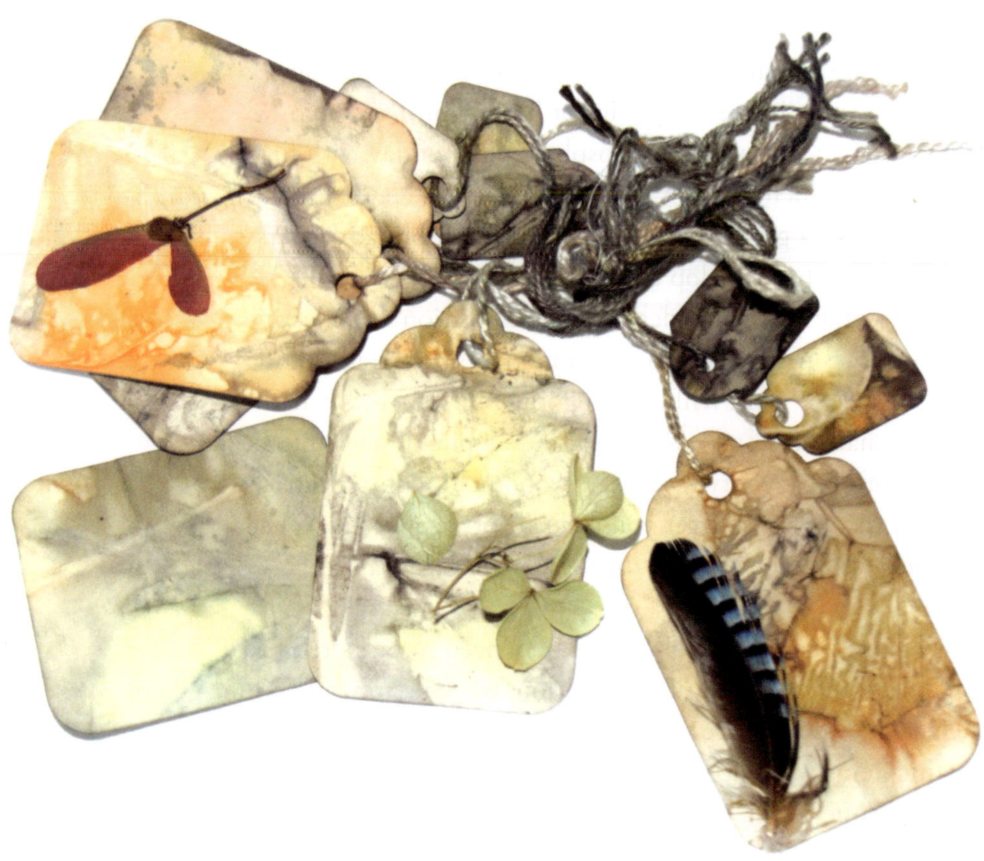

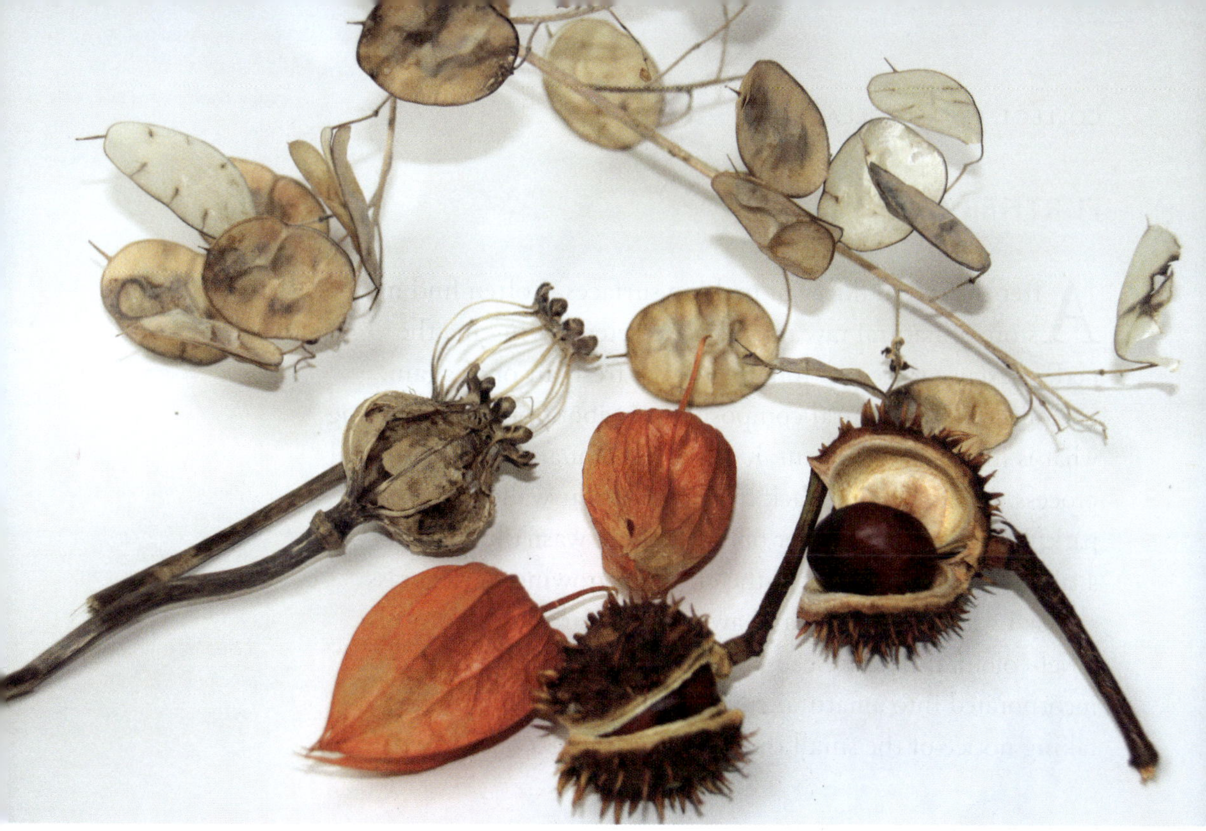

Collecting can also be an act of remembrance. Pick up coloured leaves, interesting twigs or broken bird's eggs to record a walk; capture the atmosphere of a holiday with finds from a beach such as shells, pebbles and crab's claws. Or track the seasons of a garden or allotment with samples of flowers and leaves as they develop and grow.

What comes first, the ideas for a composition or collecting? The answer is neither – or both! Sometimes, inspiration to make a piece of work will lead to going out specifically to look for more natural resources; other times, a pile of new botanical contact prints, cyanotype images or joomchi will result from a search through resources you have already collected. When, how and where one works with these materials is a very personal choice.

My gathered natural collections may need to be stored for some time before I find the inspiration, or time, to work with them. The way they are stored needs careful consideration as organic items will wither, go mouldy or simply get lost before you find time to use them. Here are some tips on storage:

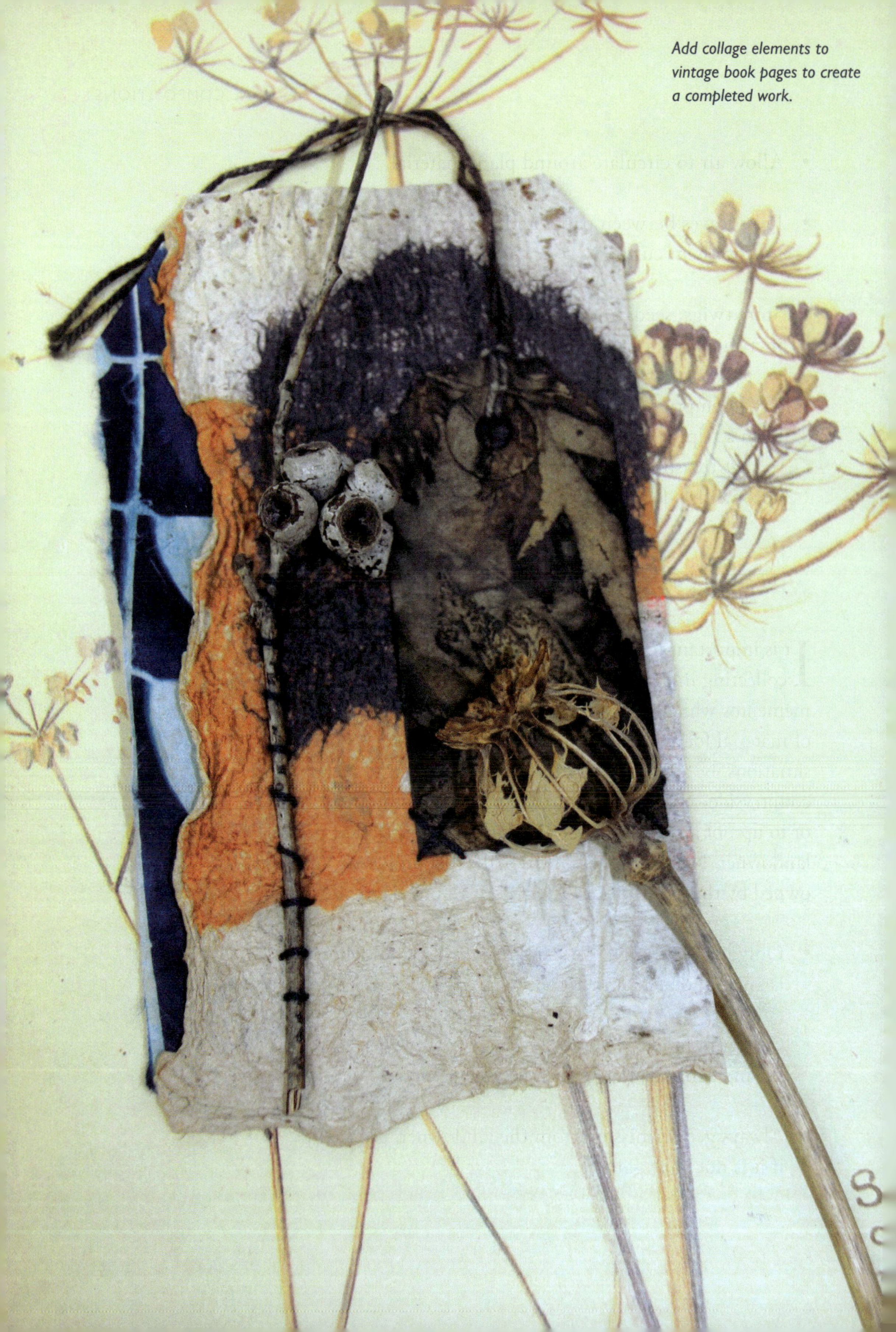

Add collage elements to
vintage book pages to create
a completed work.

- Allow air to circulate around plant material.

- Press leaves between paper and place weights on top to stop them curling.

- Store twigs, seeds and other three-dimensional items in a paper bag or cardboard box.

- Try to empty pockets and bags as soon as you return from a trip and place your finds in a labelled box so that treasured items do not get misplaced or become dry, fragile and broken.

WHEN GATHERING NATURAL MATERIAL

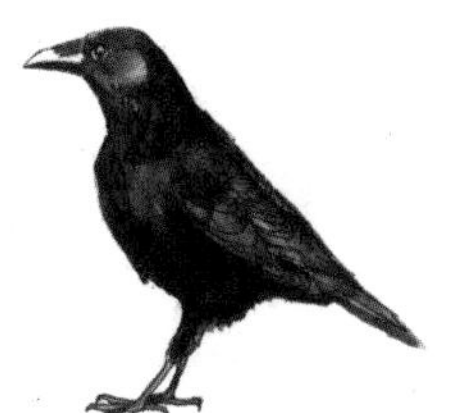

It is important to be considerate and responsible when collecting in earnest. Spontaneous collection of small mementos while on a walk is one thing; gathering quantities of material for a specific project is entirely different. For both situations, be aware of the legal protection given to plants in the countryside – it is illegal to collect protected and rare plants, or to uproot any wild plants without the permission of the landowner. Nature reserves, National Trust properties and land owned by the Ministry of Defence are all protected areas.

- Only collect things that can be identified and where there is an abundance of material.

- Collect in moderation; take no more than is necessary, leaving behind enough for the fauna to enjoy.

- Always get permission from the landowner, especially if it is not your garden.

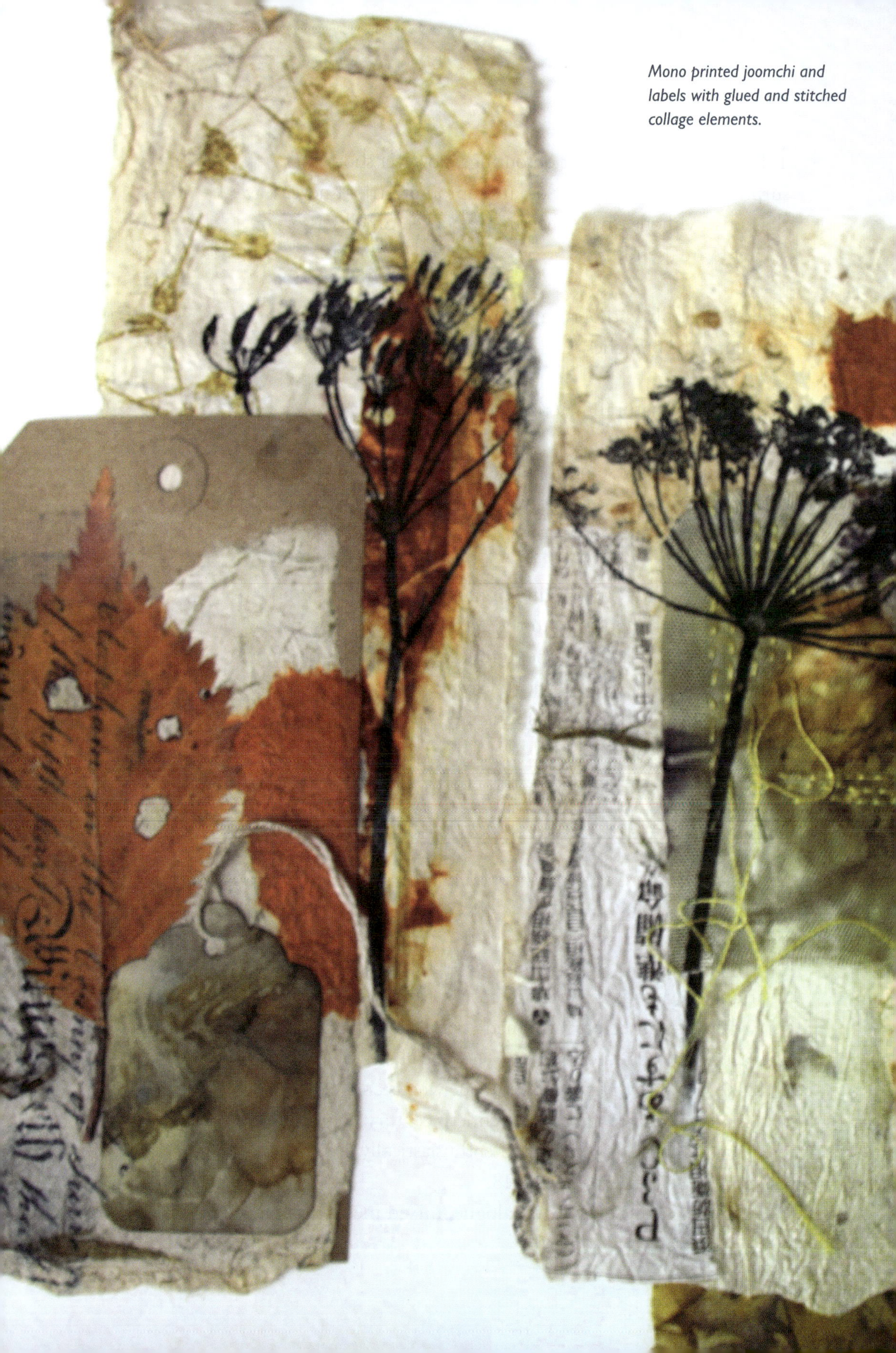

Mono printed joomchi and labels with glued and stitched collage elements.

- Take a small collecting kit on outings, however short – it's surprising what will appear on an impromptu trip. I never leave the house without a paper bag in my pocket. Small scissors or secateurs are useful.

- Collect carefully without tearing up the whole plant or damaging the branches. Use scissors or secateurs.

- Wear gloves – natural materials can be toxic.

- If you're on holiday somewhere exotic, bear in mind local restrictions on collecting and what natural items can be brought home through customs.

Incorporating gathering, foraging or collecting into an outdoor pursuit adds another purpose to the activity – even if it's just routine weeding. And, while the dramatic vistas of a landscape, a mountain range or a sea view can leave us awe struck, paying attention to small details can also inspire wonder and connect us to the natural world.

PREPARING AND WORKING ONTO SURFACES

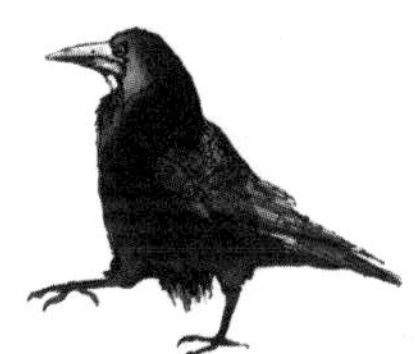

Exploring collage

The term collage describes the process of cutting, ripping and arranging various materials to create an artistic composition. It is a widely recognised art form made popular in the 1960s by Pop artists such as Andy Warhol, Richard Hamilton and Peter Blake. However, it is George Braque who is credited with introducing the form to the early twentieth century art world, where it was adopted by Picasso and enthusiastically used by the Dada movement between 1914–1918.

There are four collage types: analogue, mixed media, digital and photomontage.

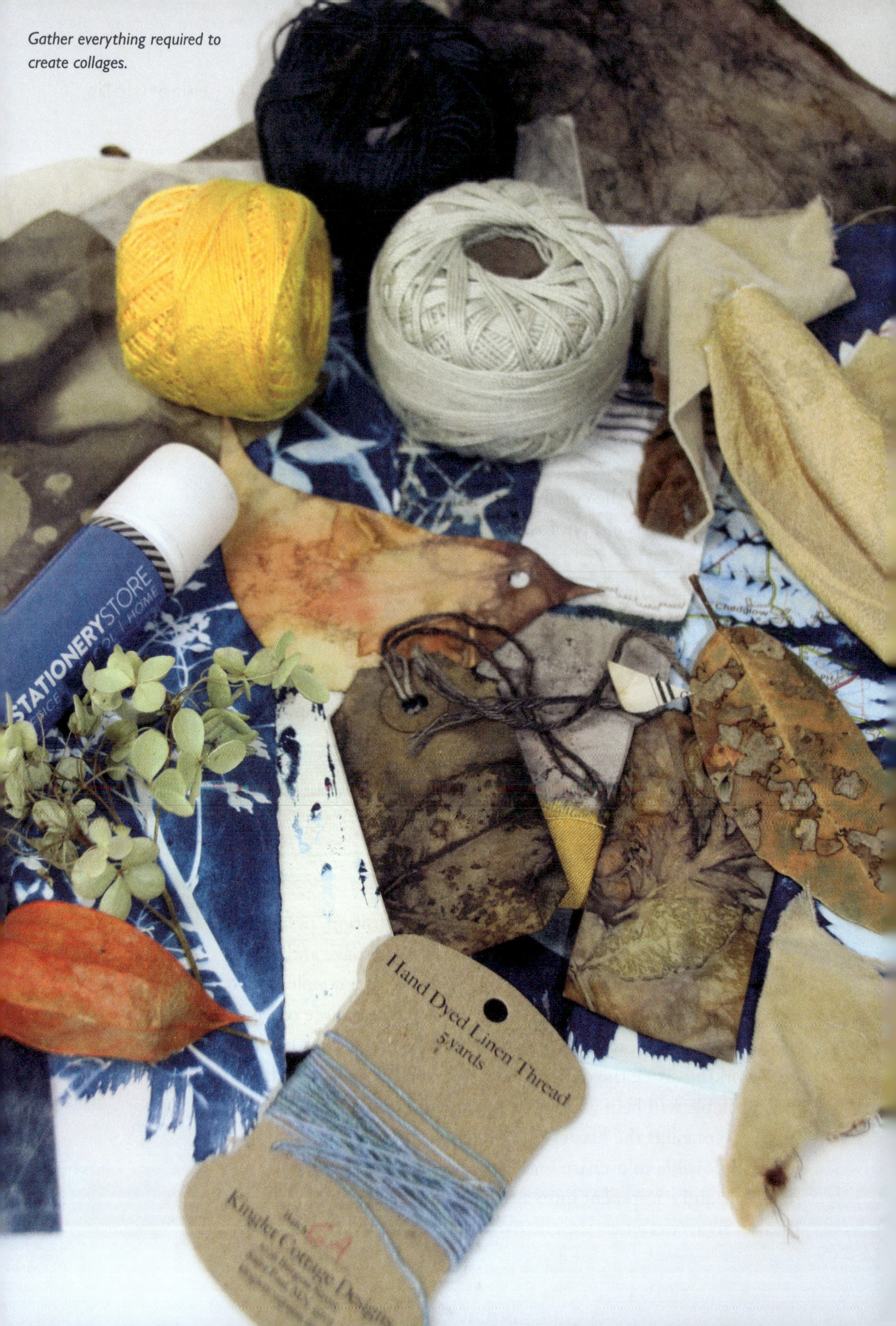

Gather everything required to create collages.

- Analogue is the manipulation of paper, fabrics and found objects that are composed and attached to a substrate to create an artistic composition. This is the most recognised collage style.

- Mixed media is the combination of analogue collage, painting and drawing.

- Digital collage uses technology to manipulate and juxtapose imagery using digital tools and software such as Photoshop. The resulting artwork is then printed.

- Photomontage is the cutting and sticking of photographic materials such as old photos.

All these collage styles offer an imaginative way to weave materials, narratives and personal creativity together. They can be used separately, or elements of each can be dipped into to enhance a composition.

This chapter explores analogue and mixed media collage techniques, however this does not preclude digital and photomontage forms; adding relevant images to a natural composition is a personal choice.

Cutting, sticking and stitching

Before you start to put together a natural composition, first prepare your inspirational materials, clear a workspace and set aside enough time to work consistently on at least a couple of pieces. It is important to have enough time to see a piece of work through to the end and not feel rushed or distracted. Setting up a working space the day before and having materials ready and available will help you make a positive start the next day. Not everyone has the luxury of a designated workspace, but it is still possible to prepare for a creative session by popping materials and equipment onto a tray, or in boxes, to make it easier to access when the creative mood strikes.

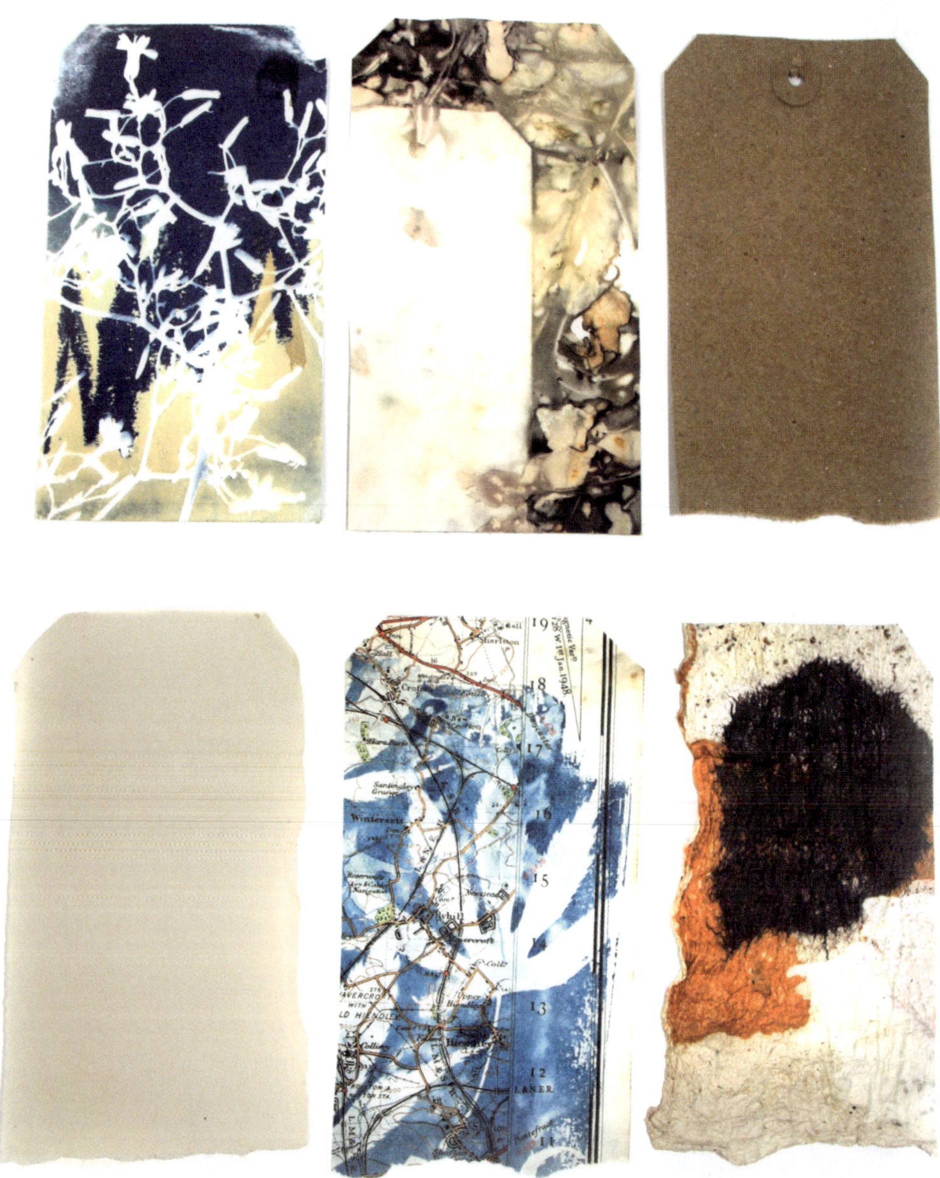

Work on several compositions at a time. Use different materials as bases. From top left to bottom right. Toned cyanotype; masked botanical contact print; manilla label; plain handmade paper; cyanotype on vintage map; joomchi.

Equipment

- Scissors for both paper and fabric
- Cutting mat
- Craft knife
- Brushes
- Needles
- Glossy magazine

Materials

- Natural surfaces i.e. botanical contact prints, cyanotype prints and joomchi
- Natural collections i.e. leaves (fresh or dried) twigs feathers, shells etc
- PVA glue
- UHU glue
- Glue stick
- Matt acrylic gel medium
- A variety of sewing threads
- A small collection of various commercial papers i.e. watercolour paper, brown paper, manilla labels
- Scraps of natural fabrics i.e. silk, cotton, wool blanket

Cutting

1 Take a piece of base paper, working in a size that doesn't feel too daunting. (Working on a smaller piece in the beginning is an efficient use of time – often a larger work takes time and materials and may not be successful.) The base paper can be a botanical contact print, cyanotype, joomchi or a commercial paper cut or ripped to size. Warm up with pieces around A5 or postcard sized. Smaller experiments while warming up to this process creates several precious works and a chance to highlight smaller collected treasures. Keeping everything the same dimensions will make for a cohesive collection. There is also something very satisfying about a group of works in a similar format. Lay out several pieces in different types of paper, working on three or four compositions at the same time. This generates more ideas and an opportunity to experiment.

2 Start to build up layers of contrasting or toning papers onto a base substrate. This could be random to begin with – a ripped piece of white paper onto a busy sheet of joomchi; a toning length of botanical contact paper onto a brown label and a cyanotype image placed onto a contrasting colour. Nothing is glued down yet, so things can be moved and rearranged. It is surprising how much decision making is used in juxtaposing these pieces and there is no right or wrong decision at this stage. It is often said that less is more, but this is not always the case; busy, intricate compositions can work well. The only thing to watch out for is that you don't lose interesting details in an overly complicated arrangement.

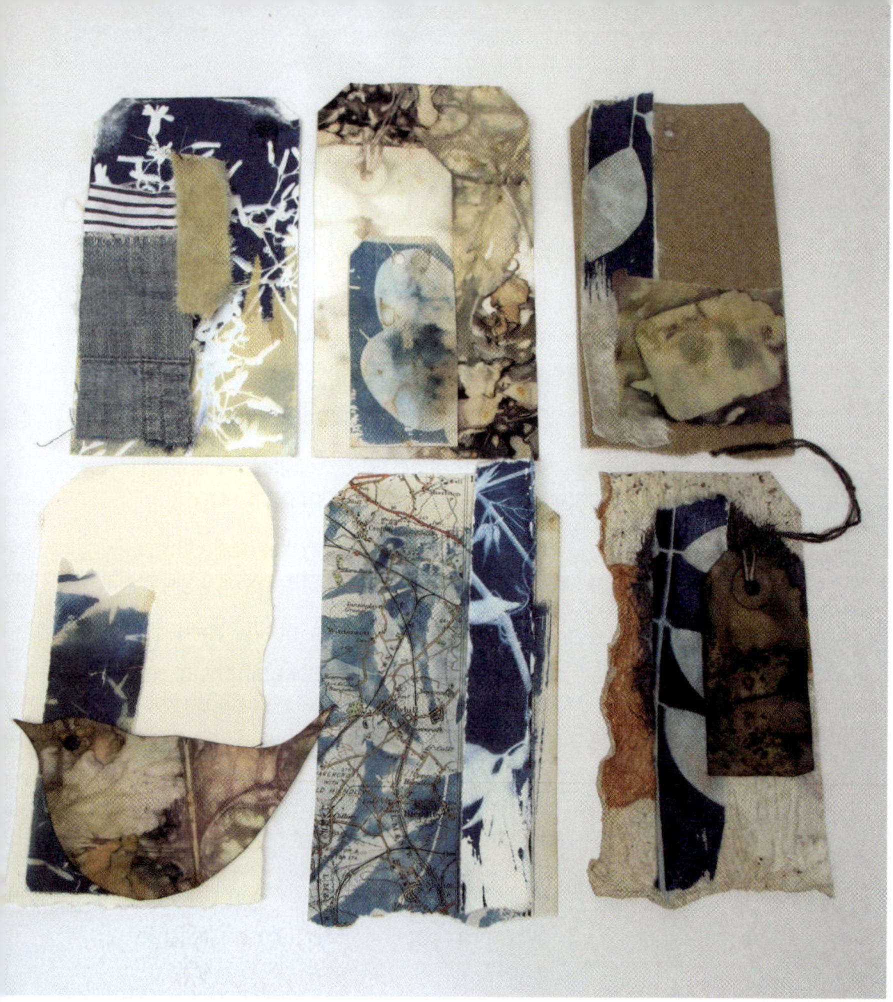

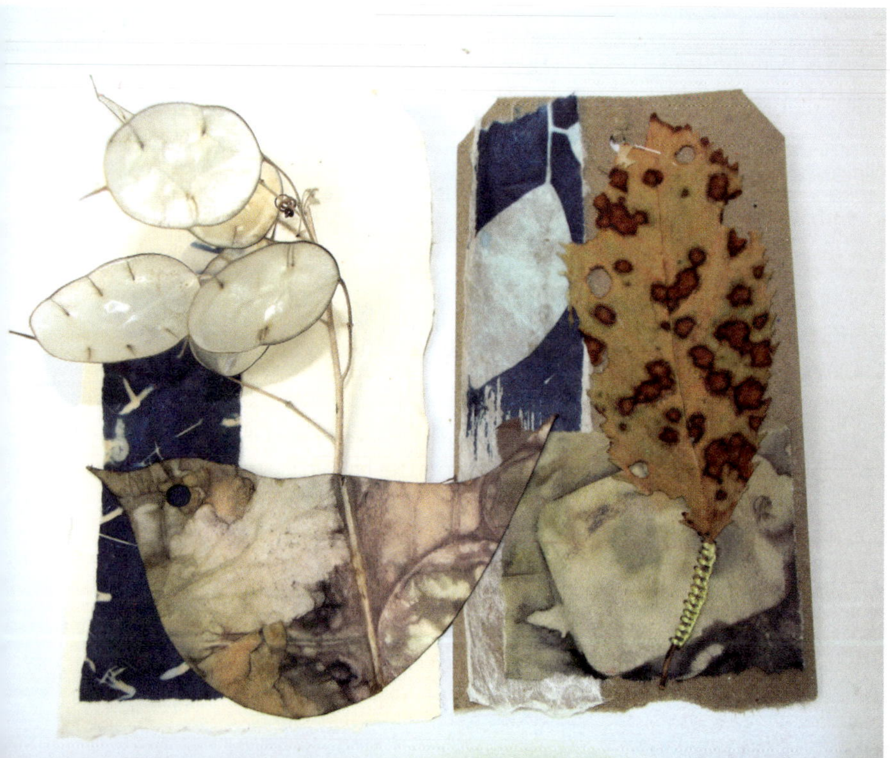

Start by placing snippets of contrasting papers onto the bases.

Attach natural elements with glue or stitching.

3   To cut or to rip edges? This is a very personal choice. A torn edge when collaging helps the edges better blend into the surface when everything is glued down, especially when using your joomchi and botanical contact papers. Care must be taken when ripping paper as it can be an unpredictable process. If a random look is required, then tear away but some papers only rip evenly in one direction and Joomchi is tough to tear, even against the edge of a ruler. Some papers will need some encouragement to give a purposeful torn edge: wet the tearing direction using a brush, then tear along the wet edge in the desired shape. With their photographic look, cyanotypes seem to lend themselves to a harder, graphic cut edge so use a craft knife or scissors to cut them, rather than tearing.

4   Create a variety of compositional styles. Leave spaces to add a collected item such as a leaf or pressed flower later. Some collages will look finished at this point and will be ready to stick down. This is a good time to consider the aesthetic of the collection: has the group become experimental with each piece looking different, or does it look like a cohesive group? The process of putting these collages together is intuitive so do not resist an emerging style. Breath into it and go with the flow. There are no right or wrong choices.

Sticking

1   Once you are happy with the collaged compositions, it's time to get everything stuck down. There is a bewildering selection of adhesives on the market, and each has its uses. To keep the creative momentum going, or if a permanent gluing option is not required at this point, start to attach the paper pieces together with a glue stick. This will keep collage pieces in place and make them easy to reposition as glue sticks remain tacky for some time – an advantage if you are undecided about positioning. However, it should not be seen as a permanent option as the glue will dry out over time and bits will become detached.

2   When the composition is as you want it and everything is ready to be permanently attached, use a good quality PVA glue. The best way to use PVA is to coat the collage pieces evenly on the reverse and then place them on the base paper. Using a glossy magazine, place the collage piece face down and glue the back, working from the middle to the edge with a glue brush. Apply the glue as evenly as possible, ensuring that the edge is well covered. Place into position on the base paper and gently massage the surface from the middle. If the glue seeps out from the edge, quickly wipe off with a damp cloth.

Fold the used magazine paper glue-side in to avoid getting PVA on the surface of subsequent collage pieces. Systematically work through your collection of compositions. Allow the glue to dry naturally, or speed things up with a hair dryer. PVA will make work feel damp when first applied as it soaks into the surface, but it dries to a strong finish. It is especially good when gluing thin papers such as tissue as it will dry clear, leaving the paper with a translucent quality. Do not be over generous at the gluing stage as PVA will leave shiny marks around the edges of pieces if it seeps out and dries. Glue brushes can be cleaned with warm water after use.

3   Once the base collages have been finalised and have dried completely, you can begin embellishing them further with three dimensional collected items. This process of arranging mirrors the initial decisions used when making the base collages. Should the additions blend or contrast with the background? With several pieces underway, there is more room to experiment and find a satisfying aesthetic. You also need to decide whether the piece will be a permanent observation or a transient record of nature where the attached item may change over time. Once the items are in place, stick them down with UHU glue, which is a liquid synthetic resin adhesive that quickly dries clear and bonds to most surfaces. As with the collage pieces, it is best to add the glue to the item rather than the surface to avoid glue stains. Hold in place until the glue bonds; this should take a matter of seconds. Always read the instructions that come with any adhesive used.

4   Feathers are an attractive addition to a collage but they are tricky to glue down. PVA, for example, makes the filaments clump unpleasantly together. The best way to attach delicate feathers is with matt gel medium. Coat the surface of the collage generously with gel medium using a soft brush, then lay the feather into the gel. Next, moving in the direction of the feather filaments, brush the medium over the feather. This will dry across the collage to a matt finish with the feather completely attached.

5   Stitching things into place is another way to secure items to collages. You are not aiming to create intricate embroideries, but to use basic stitches to attach bulkier items such as twigs, shells or small pebbles. It is also useful for items that are not flat enough to glue securely, such as feathers with thick quills, vegetation with chunky stems or undulating leaves. Attach the item with spots of UHU to hold it in place while stitching. Choose a contrasting or toning coloured thread.

Glue the thread end to the back of the collage, allow the glue to dry then, using bold stitches, sew the item into place. When working on paper, do not sew stitches too closely as this will create a perforation and the paper will tear. Joomchi's fabric-like texture makes it ideal to stitch into and it may be a better choice of surface for these natural collections. Once items are stitched to the joomchi, you can attach it as an additional element to another part of the collage to cover knots and wayward stitching on the back. If you are using a paper surface, be positive; once a stitch has been made, it will leave a hole if it's removed. However, holes can be covered with another piece of collage, or a weakened surface can also be strengthened with a glued tissue paper repair. A visible mend – either a glued or stitched patchwork piece – can enhance the final composition.

Tips when using natural materials

- Embellishing work with natural collections creates a narrative to a collage but both fresh and dried natural materials have their limitations. Fresh vegetation will change over time, losing colour and texture. Some things will dry, but other flora may dissolve. Seaside collections can often produce an unwanted smell, while twigs and bark might have hitchhikers that appear when it's warm and dry, so check everything for unwanted guests.

- It is better to stitch fresh leaves and flowers in position first and then put them under a weight to press for a few days. A fresh leaf will not tear when stitched and then will dry flat and in place. A fresh flower will hold its shape initially, but may drop petals over time.

- Dried leaves tend to crumble when stitched, although it is possible to stitch around the stem with care.

- Gently coat dried pressed leaves or flowers with matt gel medium, using a soft brush. This will stabilise the surface preventing damage and crumbling.

Creative extensions

- Stitch single items to small tags, add details such as the date, place it was found or name of the natural item. This focused detail can be added using PVA or UHU glue and will add small narratives to the collage, especially if the backgrounds are part of the same story.

- Using a fine line permanent marker or a dip pen with Indian ink, add written details of a walk, the garden or descriptions of the natural world onto white tissue or botanically contact-printed tissue. Layer sections of this into a collage or over natural collections using matt gel medium. This will fuse the tissue onto the surface, leaving the writing just visible.

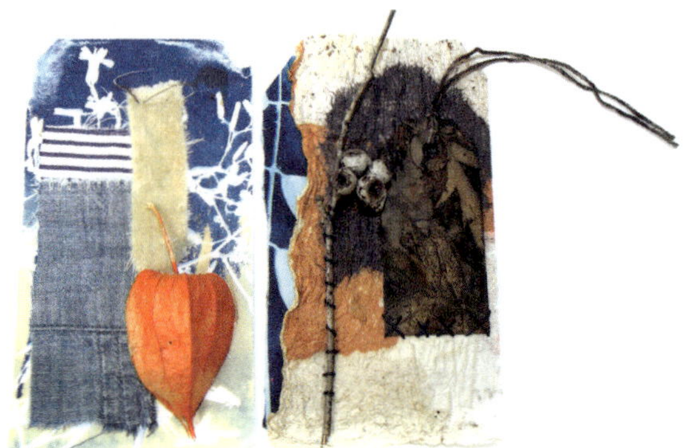

Consider contrasting colours or a subdued palette when developing compositions.

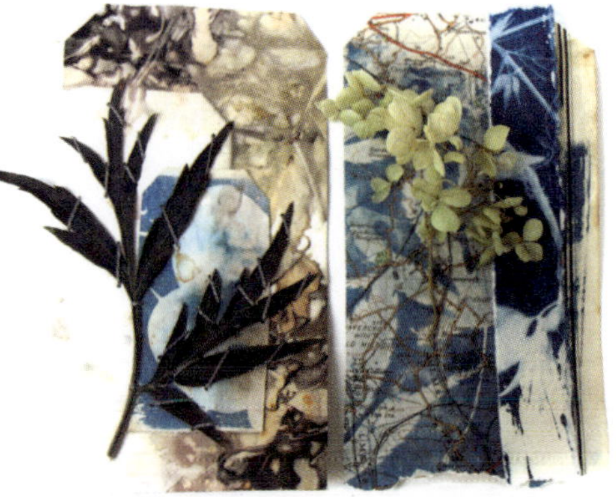

Fresh material can be stitched on. Dried pieces will successfully glue to the base.

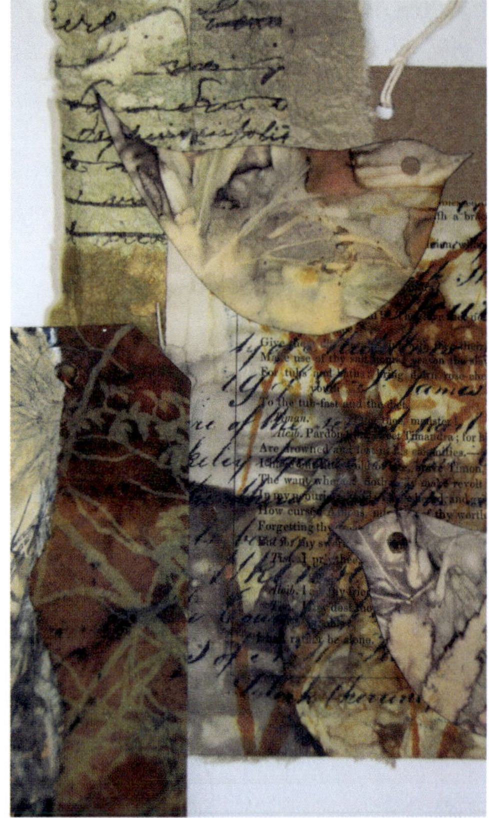

Collages can be larger with asymmetric edges. Layers of tissue paper and print are combined with botanical contact papers. Lend a narrative to the collage with a figurative element.

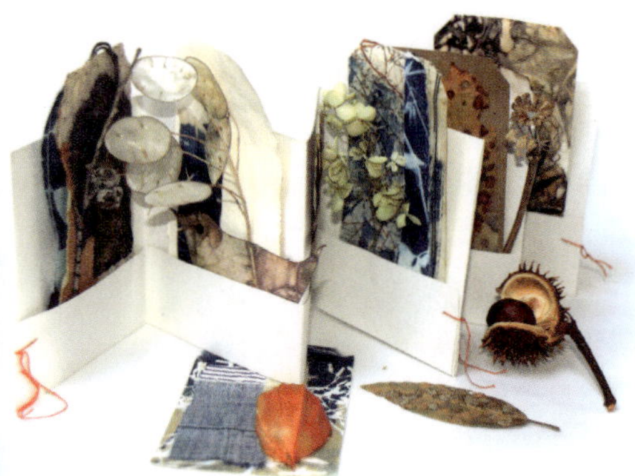

Display compositions in a pocket concertina book.

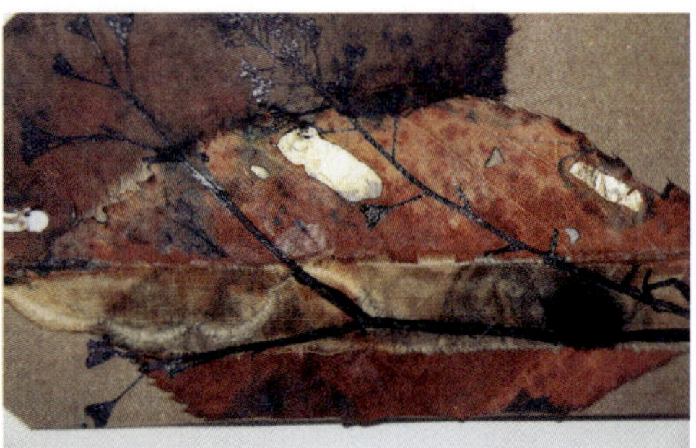

This dried pressed leaf is glued onto the base with a strip of vintage fabric attached. Pressed Shepherd's Purse (capsella bursa-pastoris) is monoprinted onto the surface.

- Stitch down any collage surfaces that have not quite bonded. This will add another texture and colour. Think about using decorative stitches such as cross stitch, French knots and running stitch in contrasting colours, making a feature of them.

- When the glue is completely dry, add mixed media elements to the collaged composition with paint and stencils. Add to the natural narrative using stencils and colours that blend with the composition. Make stencils using cereal box card and draw around found leaves, using a craft knife to cut out the shape. With a sponge and acrylic paint, dab the paint through the stencil onto the collage surface. This works well in areas of collage that need their edges disguised; a neatly placed stencilled area acts as a visual zip, blending one surface with another.

- In the spirit of mixed media, drawn and painted elements could also be added. The thought of adding observational drawing to the piece may be a step too far creatively for some, in which case a photomontage-style image may work instead, using carefully curated pictures from vintage nature books or magazines. These can either be added as an additional element or used as a base as part of the initial collage process. (This will create a strong story line to the finished piece.) Magazine images are readily available, but tend to be shiny. If so, try painting over the cutout with matt gel medium to blend it with the other papers.

At the end of this collaging process, you will have accumulated a series of finished pieces, works that need more attention and things that may be considered disposable. It is always a good idea to leave things to settle before making big changes, leaving the work out to look at for a day or two before rearranging, adding to compositions or disposing of work. It is surprising how, after some time and space, feelings can change about the work that has been done.

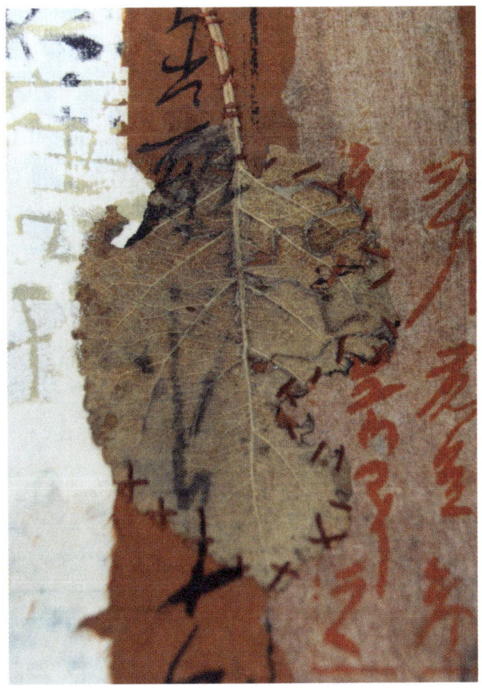

Stitch leaves into a sketchbook page — fresh leaves do not tear when stitched and dry flat.

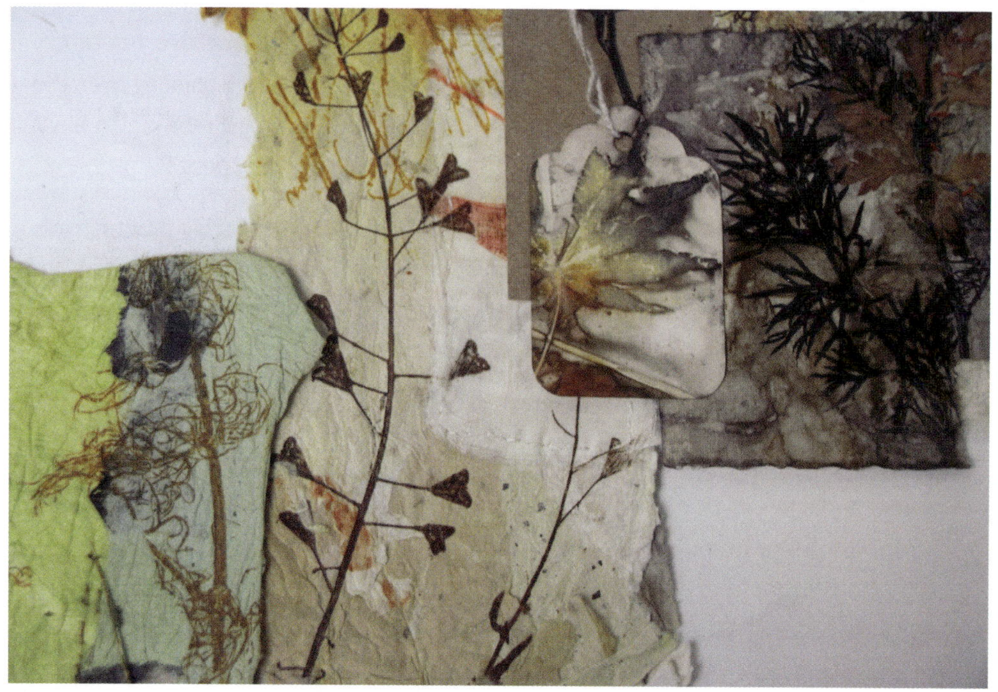

A close up of pre-monoprinted joomchi and botanical contact printed samples.

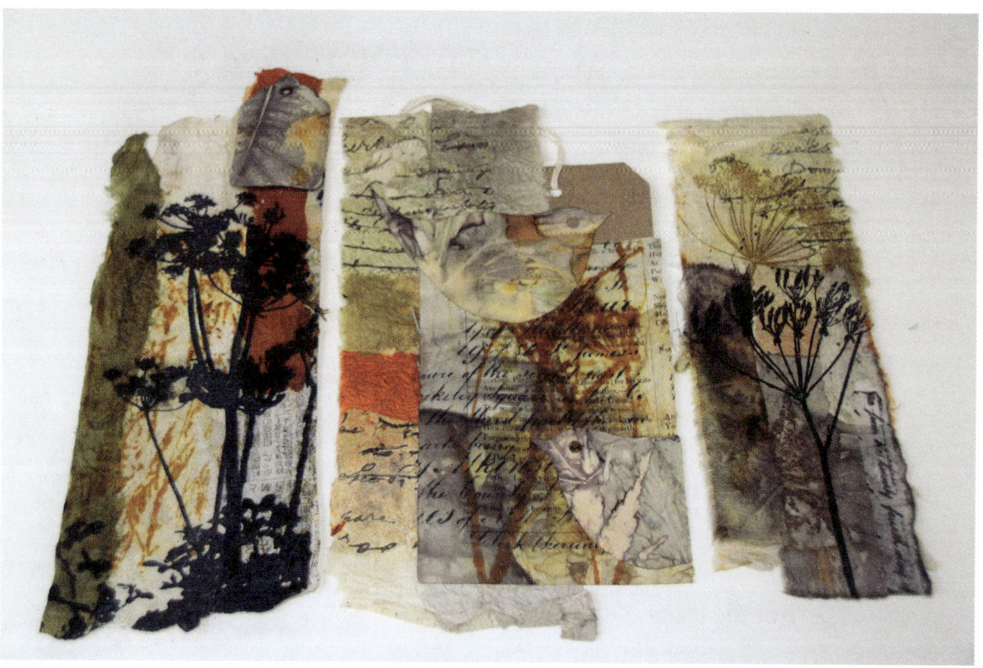

Delicious groups of collaged compositions.

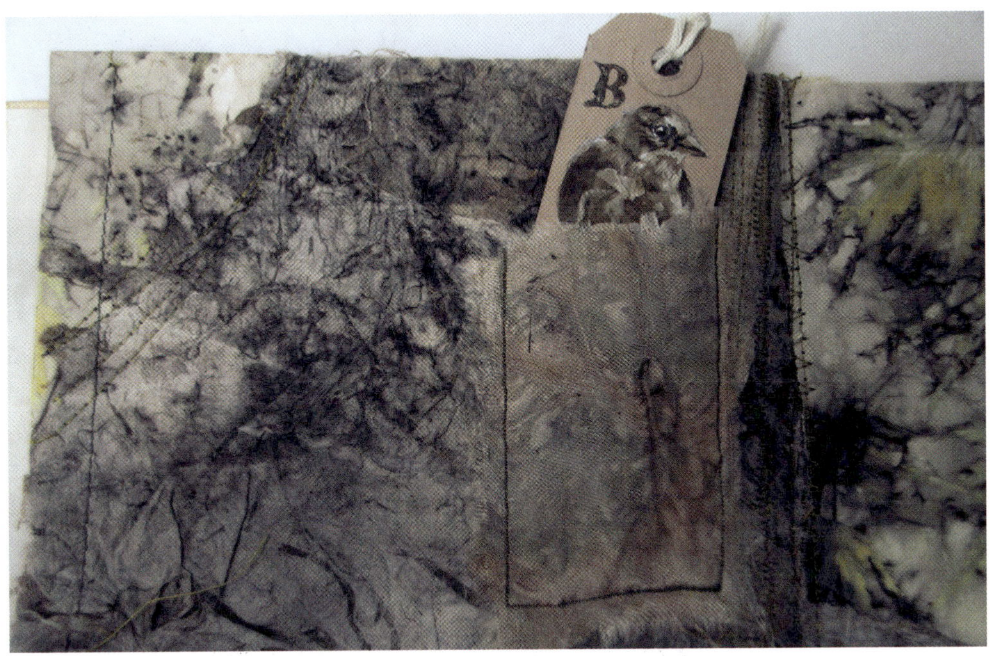

Gluing is not the only option – collaged elements can be held together using hand or machine stitching. Joomchi works well as a base to stitch into.

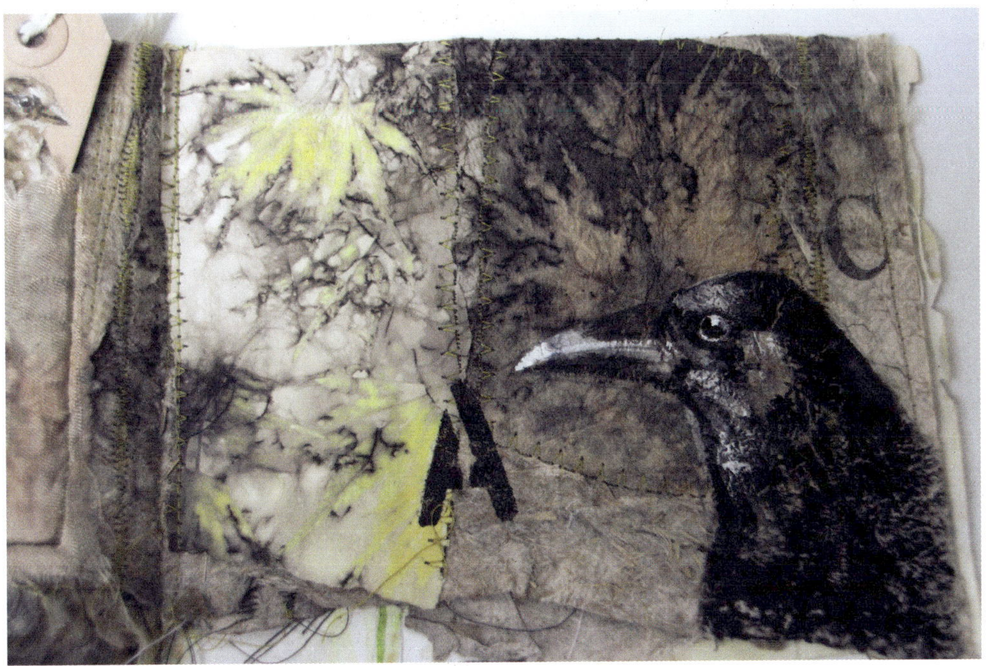

Add drawing and stencilling using collages as a base.

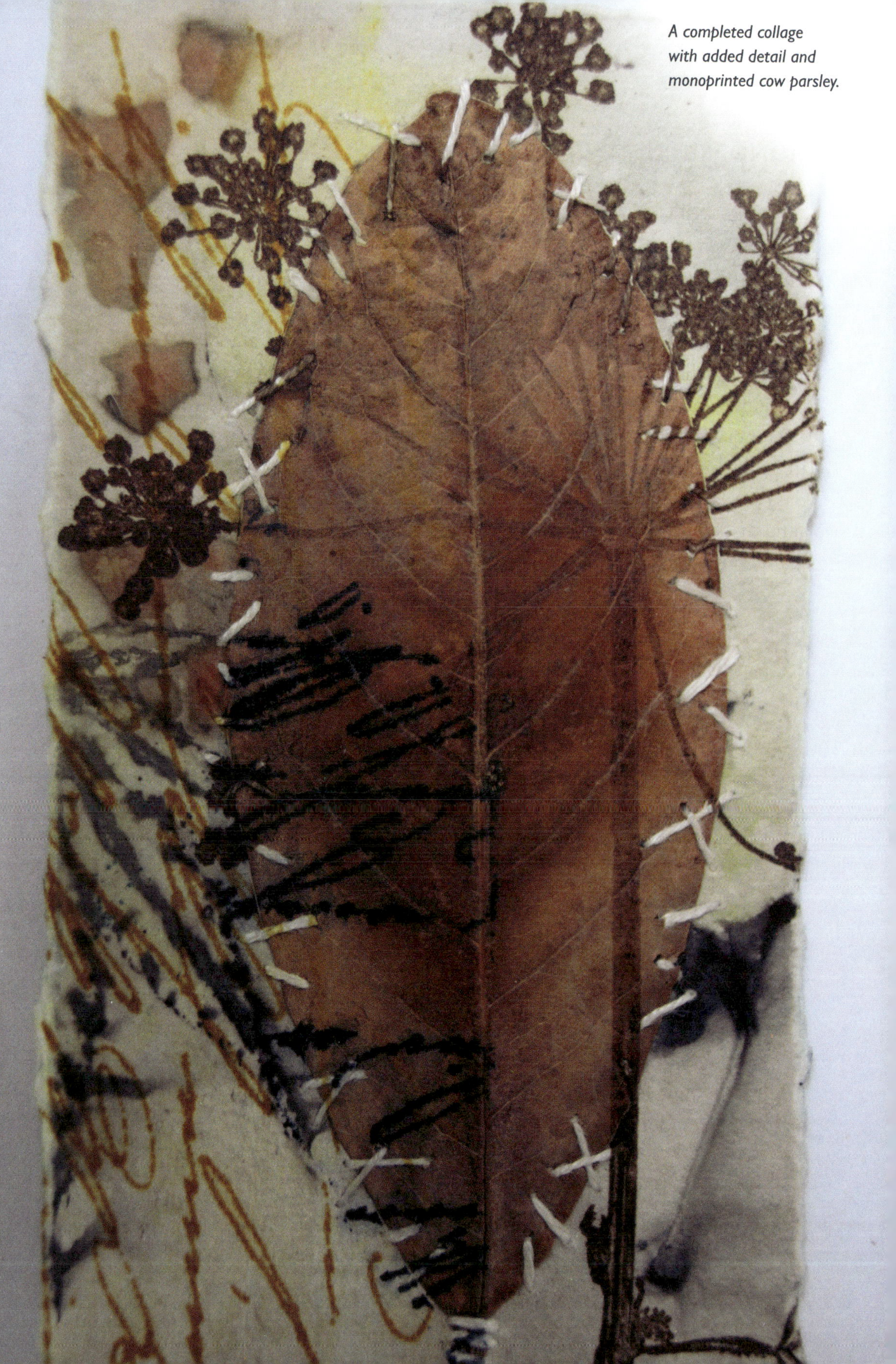

*A completed collage
with added detail and
monoprinted cow parsley.*

MONOPRINTING WITH NATURE

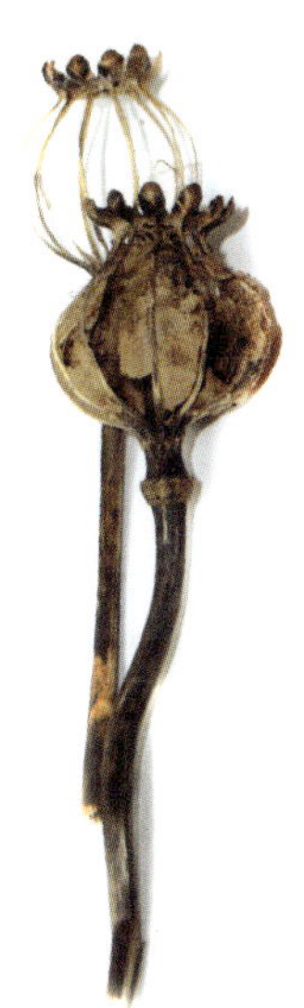

An accessible printmaking process, monoprinting can introduce graphic images to a composition with or without the use of a printing press. It allows detailed imagery to be transferred onto flat surfaces using found natural materials and is particularly good for transferring and repeating delicate copies of collected leaves and flowers onto previously made surfaces or collages.

Monoprinting should not be confused with monotypes, which are made by transferring a painted or drawn image from smooth glass or plastic surface onto paper. A monoprint, on the other hand, uses a matrix which can be inked, printed and then inked again and reprinted in a different position and colour.

Collecting and pressing vegetation

Pressed and dried leaves and plants are useful for several processes. Once you have a collection of pressed items they can be used in several different techniques. Pressed foliage is ideal to use as a mask in cyanotypes, perfect for adding to collages and can also be stitched or glued directly onto collages after they have been used to make monoprints. This allows the same resource to be used more than once, creating visual continuity.

My collections tend to be of delicate plants and leaves. I am particularly drawn to spring flowers such as snowdrops from the garden, cow parsley and other umbellifers in the summer and skeletonised leaves in the autumn. All these are fragile but, after being pressed for a couple of months, they seem to hold their own when used in printmaking.

Here are some helpful techniques to successfully dry plant matter to extend its creative life:

- Press a collection as quickly as possible after picking to preserve as much of the plant's natural shape. Some will start to go floppy soon after picking, making them awkward to position.

- Plant matter should be dry before being pressed to prevent it from going mouldy. Carefully blot damp specimens with kitchen towel or other absorbent material to take off the surface wetness.

- Check for any hitchhikers. Gently shake out the plant material to dislodge any insects and look carefully for any hidden slugs and snails.

- You don't need a flower press – although if one is available, do use it. I find it quicker and more convenient to use a large book (vintage encyclopaedias work well) which can be put back on its shelf while things are drying. Open the book, starting at the back and place the kitchen towel across the open pages. Arrange the plant material on one half of the towel, leaving space around each piece. Try not to overload the page or let items overlap. Fold the other half of the kitchen towel over the top and turn a few pages over. Keep all plant materials within the kitchen towel so that it doesn't

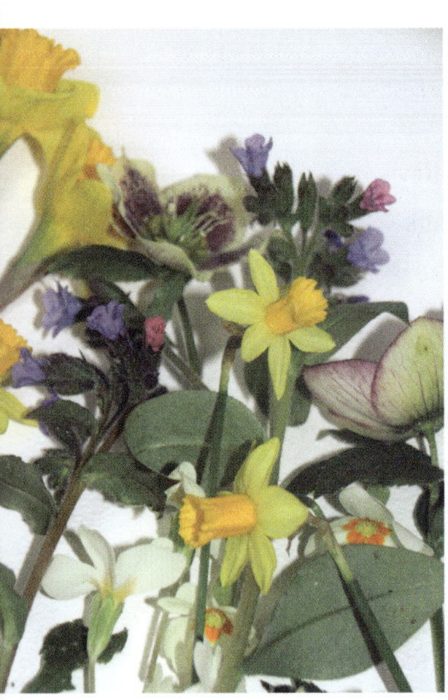

Collecting flowers to press in spring.

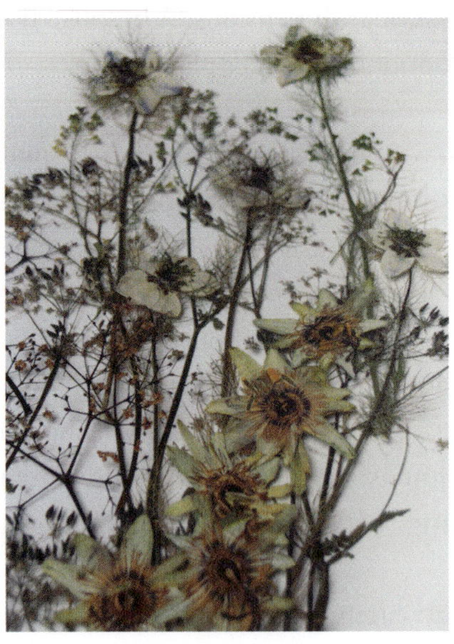

Flowers collected and pressed in the summer.

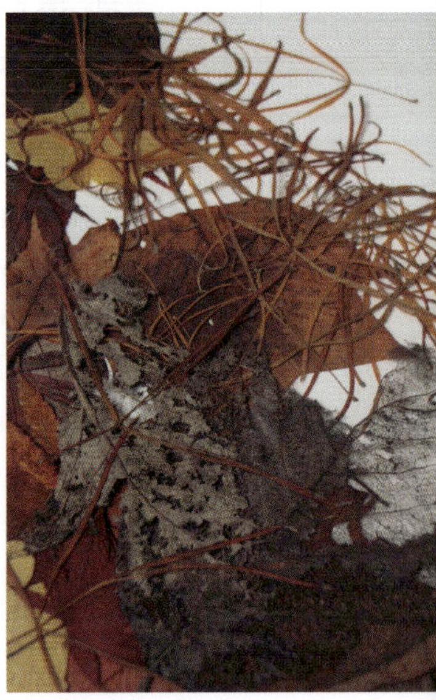

A variety of leaves collected in autumn.

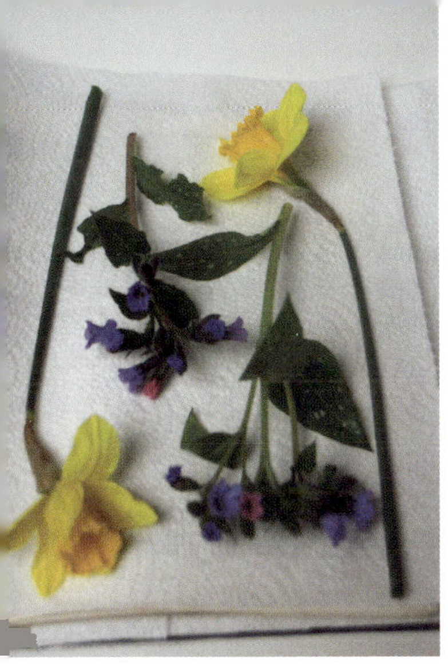

Lay flowers and leaves
between kitchen towels.
Space well apart.

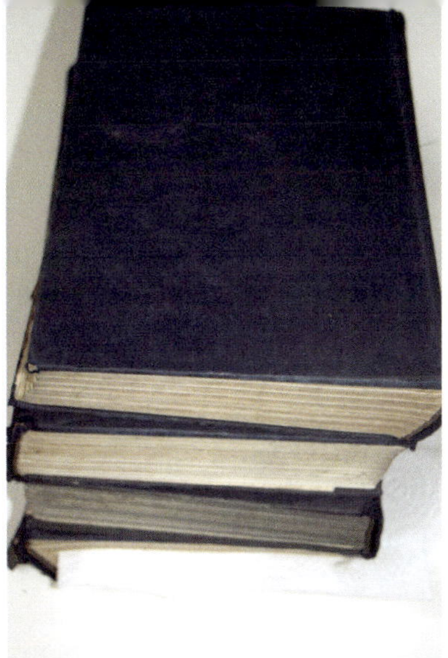

Press leaves and flowers
using large books.

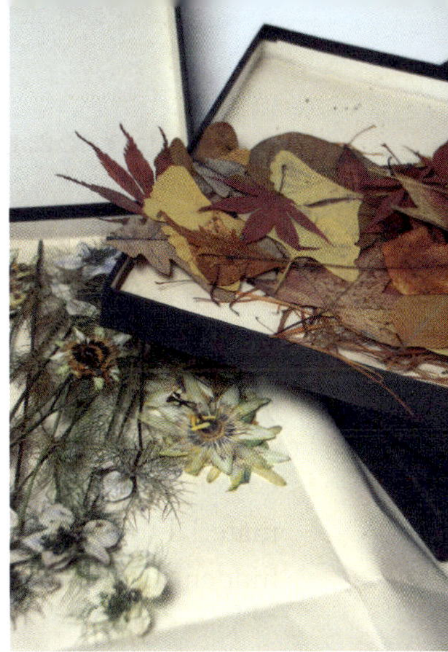

Dried and pressed
collections can be stored
in cardboard boxes.

mark the pages of the book and make sure there are no stems sticking out as they may get caught and dislodge the plant when the book is returned to the shelf.

- Avoid plants and leaves that have thick, woody stems and flowers with thick, fleshy centres. Both will stop the book closing properly and prevent thinner plants pressing successfully. Try to use plants with similar dimensions. A bespoke flower press may be a better option for thicker plant samples.

- Drying times – whatever pressing device you use – will vary depending on what is being preserved. Most delicate things will take two to four weeks but it will not hurt to leave the collection for longer. (Pressed plants are often forgotten and then rediscovered by happy chance months, or even years, later.) For the impatient, pressing a thin specimen will take just a few days, but using samples too soon will shorten the printing life of the plant as it will start to disintegrate more quickly than something that has completely dried out.

- When everything is dry, carefully collect these delicate resources, place them loosely between tissue paper and pop them in a cardboard box to wait in anticipation for the next stage.

Monoprinting: Inking up and printing delicate pressed and dried leaves and flowers

Equipment

- 2–3 rollers
- Smooth plastic surface or piece of toughened glass to act as an inking slab
- Scissors
- An etching press for textured substrates

Materials

- A variety of substrates to print onto, including collages of joomchi, botanical contact printed papers and cyanotypes
- A collection of pressed dried plant material
- Newspaper
- Glossy magazine
- A4 clear plastic presentation binding covers, 250 microns thick
- Oil based etching ink (do try other printmaking inks too)
- Cooking oil to clean up oil-based ink
- A collection of cotton jersey material for rags

The aim is to ink up the delicate dried plants, leaves and flowers and transfer a detailed image onto the paper collection and previously made collages. Using an inked acetate to transfer ink to thin delicate petals and fine stalks, rather than inking them up directly with a roller, prevents specimens breaking up, sticking to the inked roller and contaminating the ink slab with bits of dried plant matter. This inking method also seems to make the specimens last longer, prolonging their usefulness when making a piece of work.

Gathering everything together before starting will make the process easier.

1   Protect the working area with sheets of newspaper to keep surfaces clear of ink. Lay out the inking slab, the magazine to ink up on and have paper ready to print onto. Create enough space to move from inking to printing without feeling cramped. You also need somewhere out of the way to place your finished wet prints.

2   Put a quantity of ink at the top of the inking slab. Dip the roller into the ink, then roll on the slab until the roller is evenly coated. The surface of the ink should look like suede and make a hissing sound as the roller passes over it (If it doesn't, it means there is not enough ink on the roller to transfer to the binding cover.) Lift and roll the roller in one direction to achieve an even coverage. Rolling backwards and forwards will only ink up half the roller.

3   Place the binding cover onto the glossy magazine and apply the ink to the middle of the sheet, rolling up one way and holding the bottom of the binding cover. Rolling in one direction prevents the binding cover sticking and pulling up with the roller. The magazine makes the surface being inked softer and more flexible and keeps the working area clean should the roller overshoot the acetate. Do not ink right up to the edges of the binding cover; leave a clean edge to make it easier to handle the inked sheet and to keep your hands clean.

4   Lay down several thin layers of ink, building up an inky surface with the roller. Pick up the binding cover from time to time and look through the ink by holding it up to the light. If you can see pin holes of light through the inked surface then apply more ink until the coating is opaque.

5   When there is an even coat of ink on the plastic sheet, put it onto a firm, flat surface and start to arrange the dried specimens on top, placing them pattern-side down. Leave the stalks on the ink-free area so that it is easier to pick the plants out of the ink after processing. Try to fit as many samples on as possible without overlapping. Give the specimens space.

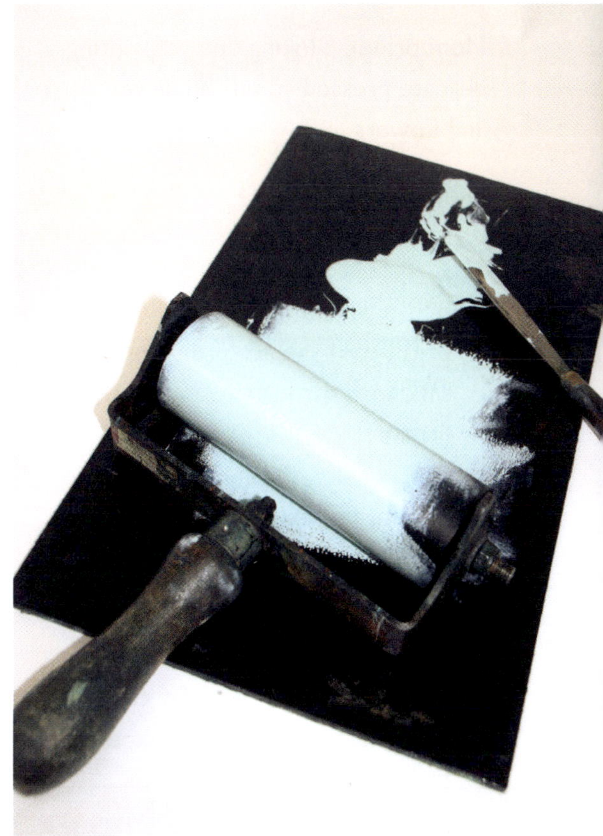

Roll ink out until the roller is evenly covered.

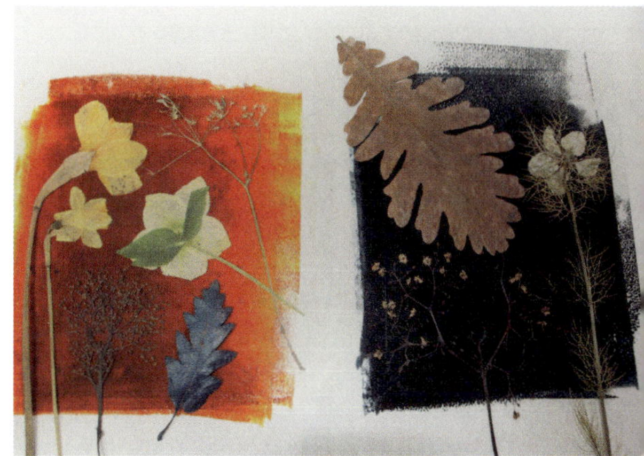

Lay dried flowers and leaves face down onto inked surface. Raw sienna on the left. Blue grey on the right.

6   Cover the inked sheet and plants with a single sheet of glossy magazine or scrap paper and roll firmly over the top with a clean roller. Apply firm, even pressure. To get more ink into delicate shapes, push the paper surface in with your fingers and massage gently. If you have an etching press, pass the acetate and magazine sandwich through it once to make firm, even contact between the ink and samples. Press lightly to avoid destroying the pressed samples.

7   Remove the paper and carefully ease off the plants. Tweezers may make this easier. One side of each piece should now be covered in ink. Be aware that fragile samples may not have survived this process.

8   Place the leaf or plant ink-side down on the receiving surface. Cover with a new sheet of glossy magazine and roll over firmly with a clean roller. This will transfer the ink from the vegetation to the chosen surface. For extra printing contact after rolling, press down firmly with your fingers, keeping the sheet of magazine in place to avoid smudging. If you have a press available, pass everything through it once for extra contact.

9   Repeat stages 4, 5 and 6, reinking the acetate and using the same pressed vegetation until it becomes too fragile to be reused.

10 Some specimens will take this printing process repeatedly and can even be stored for further use, while other plant material might come apart on the first print. It is always surprising to discover what delicate-looking materials prove to be robust. Experimentation is the key.

11 If fragments of vegetation break off into the inked acetate, scrape them off with a knife or piece of firm card before reapplying more ink.

Cleaning up

Printmaking is messy but the thought of tidying up should never be an obstacle to using certain materials or methods. Here are some very simple tips to make clearing away after using oil-based ink stress free:

- Give yourself time and space and try to print for longer than it takes to set up and clear away after a creative session.

- Have plenty of newspaper and cotton jersey rags available (old t-shirts are ideal), together with a bottle of cheap cooking oil. I always decant cooking oil into a labelled washing up liquid bottle to control the flow of oil onto a surface.

- Scrape all excess ink from the inking slab and roll the roller out several times onto newspaper to remove excess ink.

- Pour cooking oil onto the ink slab and cover the roller too. Pay attention to the edges of the roller.

- Pour and rub oil into the ink, both on the slab and the roller and rub with a cloth to emulsify it, then wipe the oil off the surfaces with a clean, absorbent cloth. Unlike white spirit, cooking oil does not dissolve the ink, it just moves it around. Cotton jersey or t-shirt material absorbs the oil and wipes it away effectively.

- Now wash everything in warm, soapy water to remove grease and blot dry.

Creative Extensions

Monoprinting plant collections onto sheets of plain paper can be a complete activity. Printing and over-printing a collection of leaves and flowers as a permanent record of a walk or season's growth in the garden or allotment can be both satisfying and inspire further creative ideas. These prints can be used as part of a collaged natural composition, or be printed directly onto a collage to add graphic detail to the composition.

- Printing onto a variety of papers can change the look of the piece. It is best to use smooth surfaces as this will pick up the fine detail of delicate vegetation. Textured substrates do not allow a detailed print of fine vegetation. Smooth papers work better for this process. Manila parcel labels are very pleasing and work well when incorporated into a collaged composition.

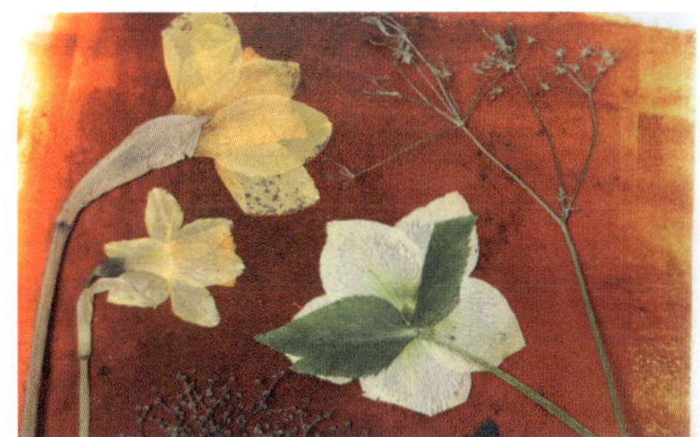

Pressed vegetation face down on the ink on the acetate sheet.

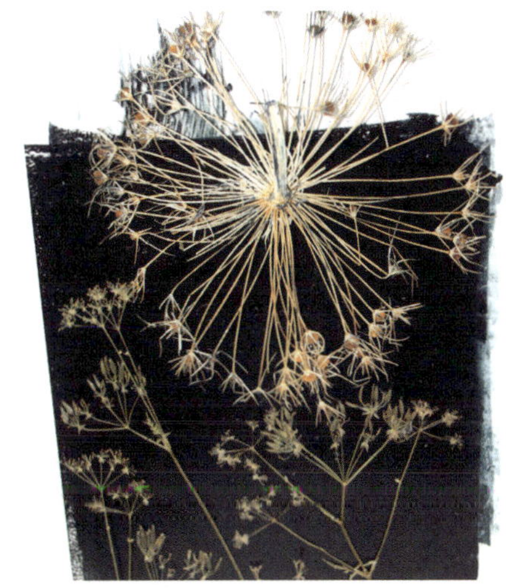

Leave a stalk or edge free to make it easier to lift out of the ink.

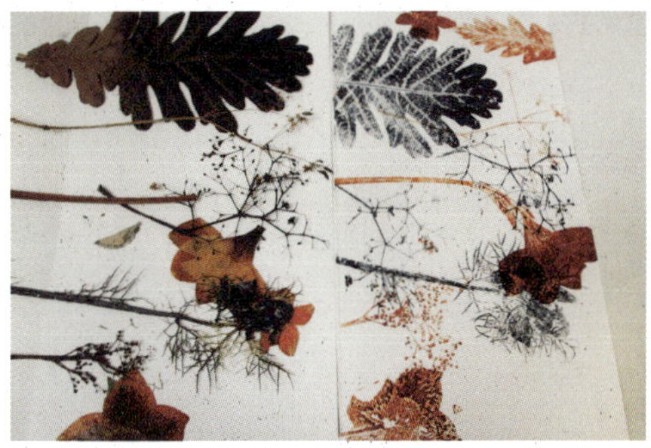

Some dried samples survive the printing process better than others.

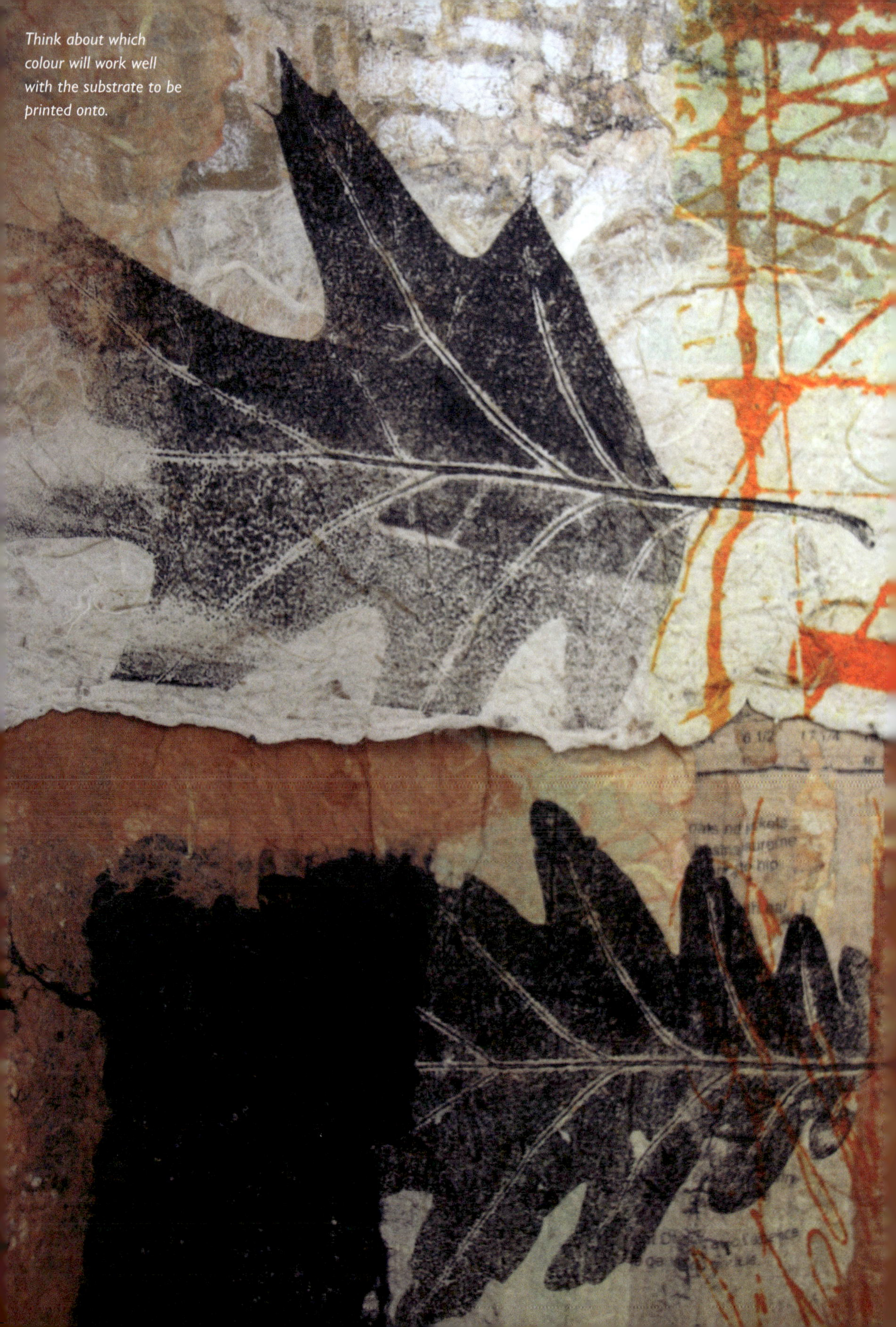
Think about which
colour will work well
with the substrate to be
printed onto.

- Consider the colour of the ink to be used. A bold sepia, black or Prussian blue, for example, will show the detail of the printed texture on most plain or patterned surfaces, while raw sienna or earthy greens will blend the image into the background – ideal when a subtle hint of a leaf texture here and there is called for. Colour choices are very personal, and it can be overwhelming, so start out with a couple and allow the backgrounds to add more colour.

- Think about the surface you are printing onto. Botanical contact papers are very colourful and seem to absorb subtle colours such as raw sienna completely so it is better to choose a bold, dark colour. Using a pressed version of a plant that has also been used in the boiling bundle will give a piece a sense of continuity.

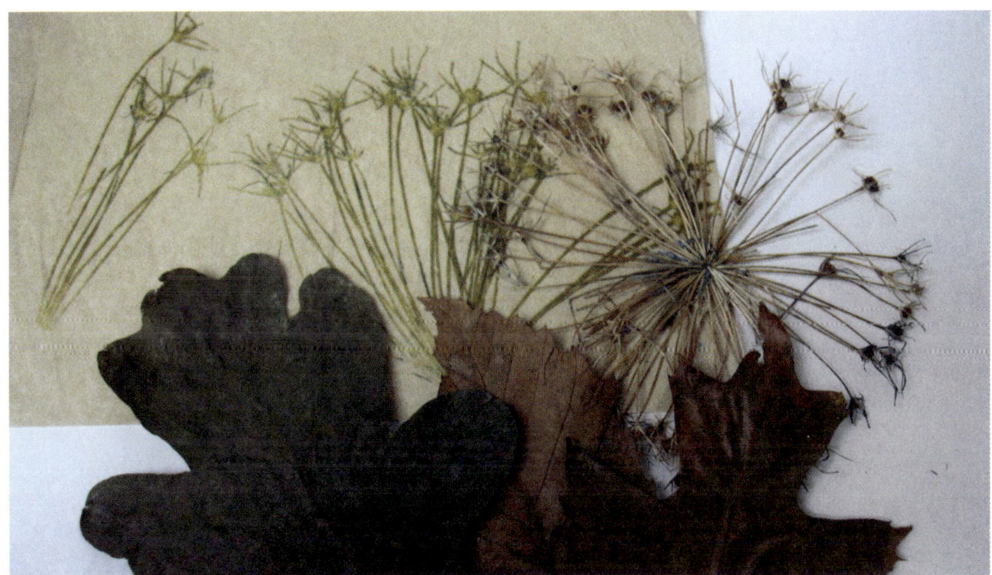

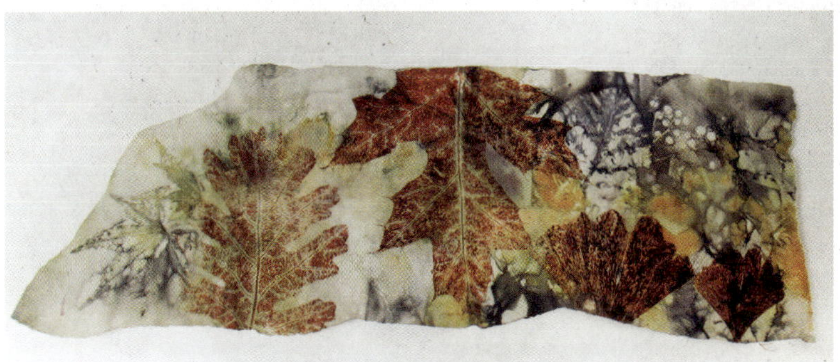

The more robust the sample the more prints can be taken.

Leaves monoprinted in raw sienna onto a botanical contact print.

- Joomchi and overlapping pieces of collage need extra pressure when monoprinting as the surface texture and joins will disrupt the printing surface. This can result in a less detailed print. This partial print may be desirable but if a clear, detailed print is what's needed, then give it an extra press using your fingers and gently massage the ink into the surface. An etching press is ideal for printing onto fabric, sheets of joomchi and textured collages as it will give firm contact between the inked surface and the substrate. Printing onto most surfaces is both quick and effective using a press. Place the collage onto the press bed, arrange the inked flowers and leaves ink side down onto the receiving surface and cover with glossy magazine paper to protect the blanket. Pass everything through the press once. This will create a strong detailed print every time.

- Because it is possible to transfer printed vegetation successfully using a roller or the back of a wooden spoon, rather than a press, printing can also be part of a sketchbook practice. Starting pages with a printed image to work on, or adding prints to a journal or diary to illustrate entries, can add an extra dimension.

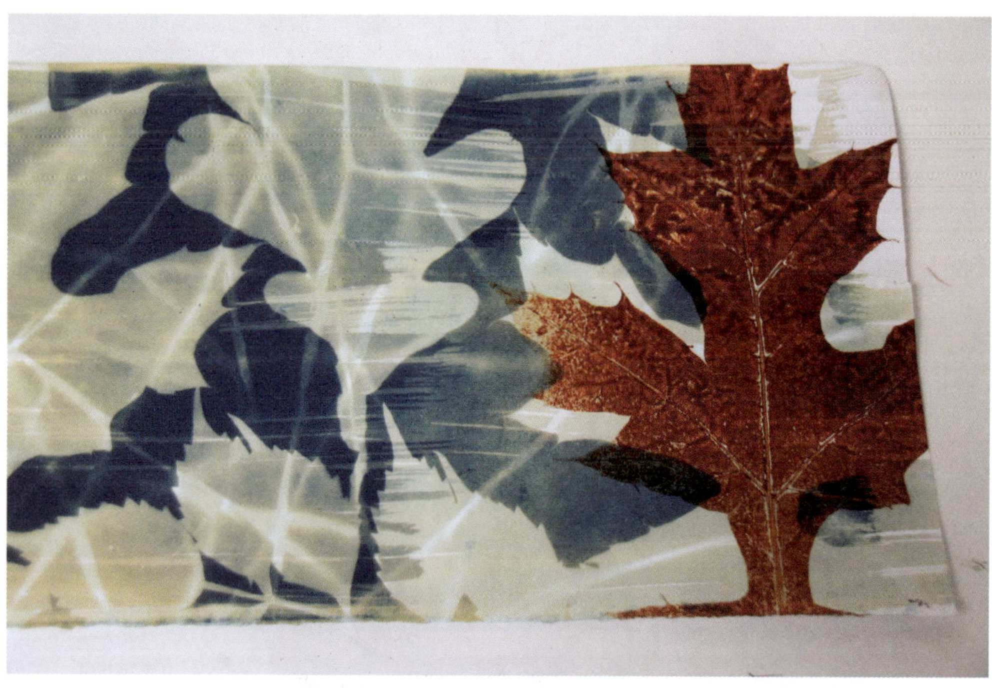

Combine techniques. This leaf is monoprinted onto a cyanotype.

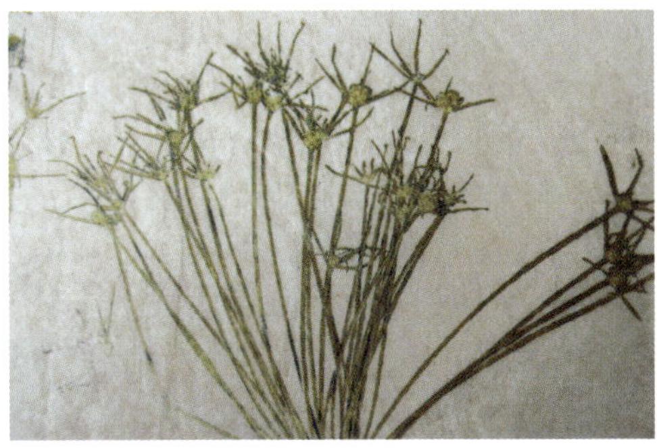

Print onto thin paper. This can be used for collage.

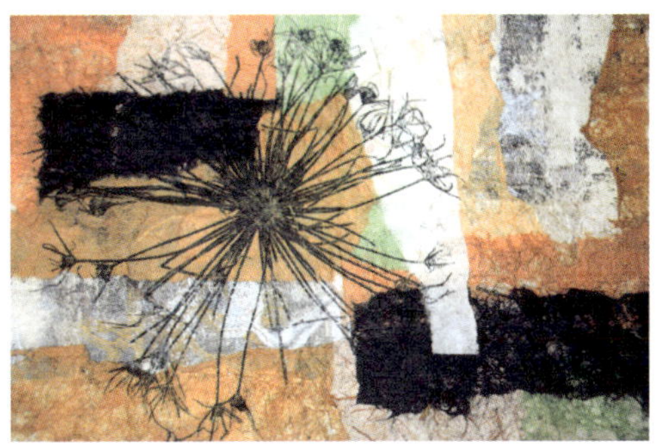

A monoprinted allium on a joomchi base.

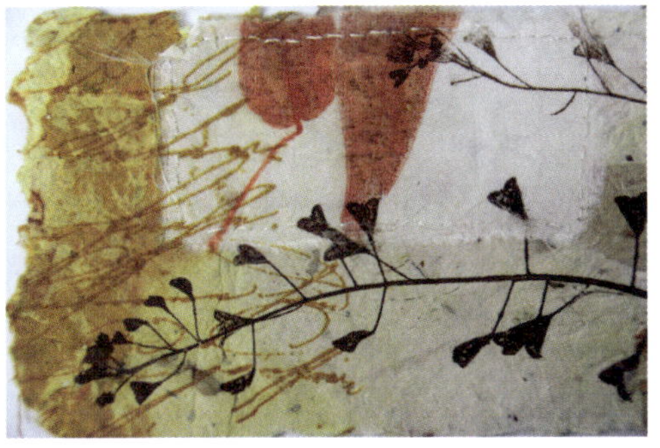

Stitched fabric onto joomchi monoprinted with Shepherd's Purse.

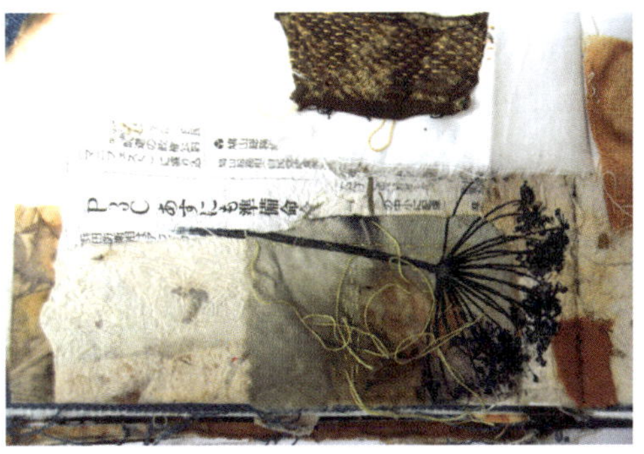

After stitching and gluing collage elements together, add a graphic hit with a monoprinted cow parsley.

- I use oil-based etching ink to print with because it gives me the coverage – and therefore the detail – I need from my pressed collection. It also dries to a waterproof surface making it possible to wash the image with watercolour paint or ink to add depth and colour. However, it is always worth experimenting with other materials and embracing the variety of the results. Sometimes we must think like chemists rather than artists to anticipate how our materials will react in certain situations.

COLLECT, PRESS, PRINT

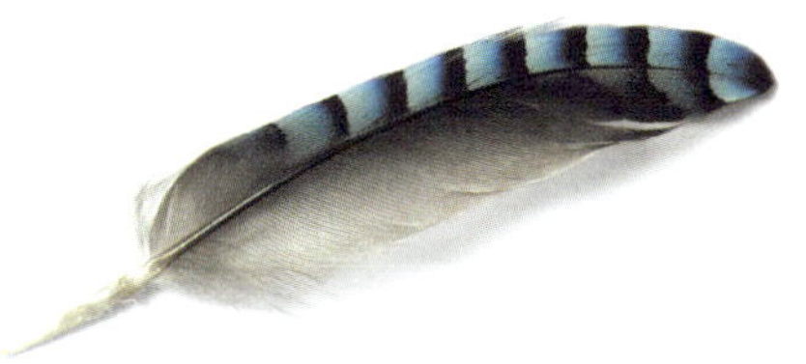

UNFAMILIAR WAYS OF SEEING

JILL WALKER

The work starts with objects found or collected, and then shaped by Jill Walker's background in weaving and teaching. Her lifelong exploration of craft focuses on handmade objects and incorporates techniques such as threading, knotting, binding, weaving and stitching into an intuitive creative process. She exhibits widely and works in Cheshire, United Kingdom.

Art-making for me is deeply emotional; it manages to reach into those hidden spaces that speak of childhood. I find inspiration while walking alone, taking the time to slow down and empty my head. I am naturally drawn to the overlooked – there's a melancholy and sense of otherness that resonates with me. I will rescue a bunch of pine needles washed down the lane after a rainstorm and gather grasses that have strayed from meadow to roadside. My work seeks to bring quiet attention to the 'small things' in nature, to find unfamiliar ways of seeing their beauty and resilience.

I spent my childhood in the post-industrial landscapes of Cheshire, where decaying chemical works and old salt mines run alongside dairy farms and working canals intertwine with meandering rivers. As kids, we would explore overgrown paths and marginal spaces on the fringes of town – areas often referred to as *edgelands*. Nature has a resilience in these places; grasses and so-called weeds run wild and gnarly trees and shrubs are able to do their own thing without fear of being pruned or manicured.

I continue to be fascinated by these places where the land reveals traces of the past, its social history and sense of purpose. I want to feel a connection to the land: to wander desire lines;

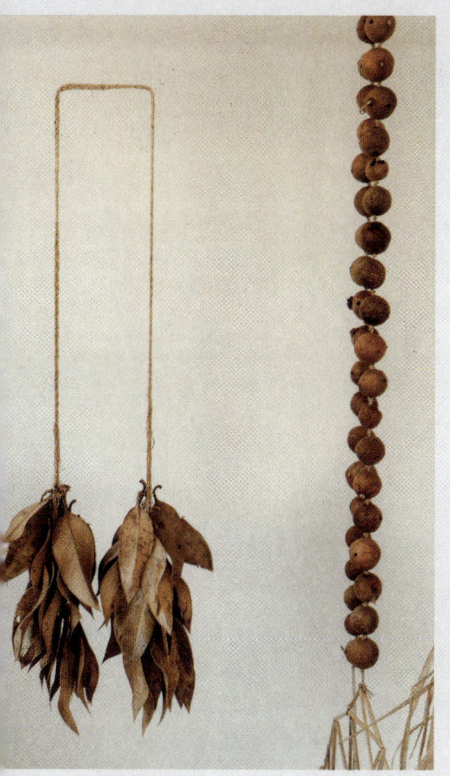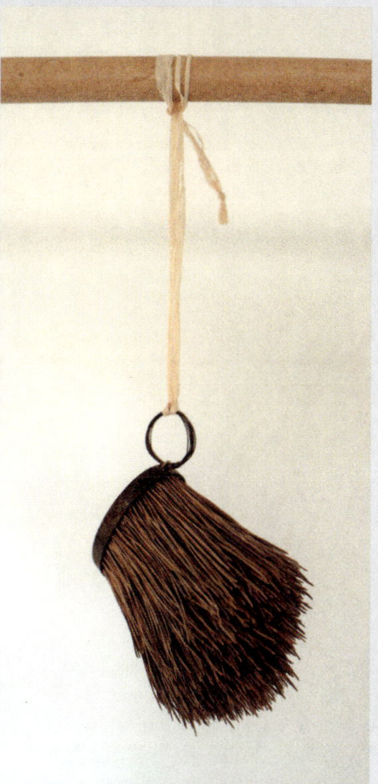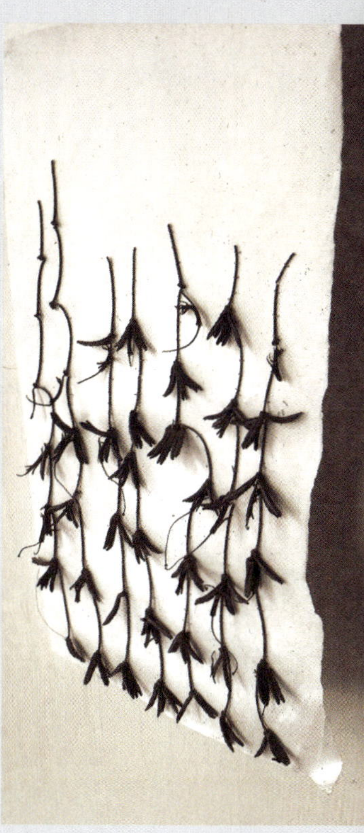

L to R Studio wall with leaves, natural dyed silk, oak galls, grass; Keep, pine needles, tin lid. 2019 (Photos Esme Mai); Rhododendron seed heads stitched to handmade paper (Photo Jill Walker).

to know the landmarks, fields and boundaries; to know its flora and fauna, its folklore and traditions.

Once back in the studio, materials collected on walks begin new conversations, taking their place alongside other treasures, both made and found. I am a collector: I love observing and orchestrating the ever-changing landscape of the studio wall, pinning playful experiments next to old postcards, drawings and photographs. The curatorial practice of arranging – considering each piece in relation to the next – gives me such pleasure and lends a sense of completion to my artistic process.

I have always been drawn to the beauty and skilfulness of hand-crafted objects, spending many hours poring over ethnographic collections, from the Pitt Rivers Museum in Oxford, England, to the Museum of International Folk Art in Santa Fe, USA. In the studio, I am the curator of my own 'museum' of artefacts and curious objects.

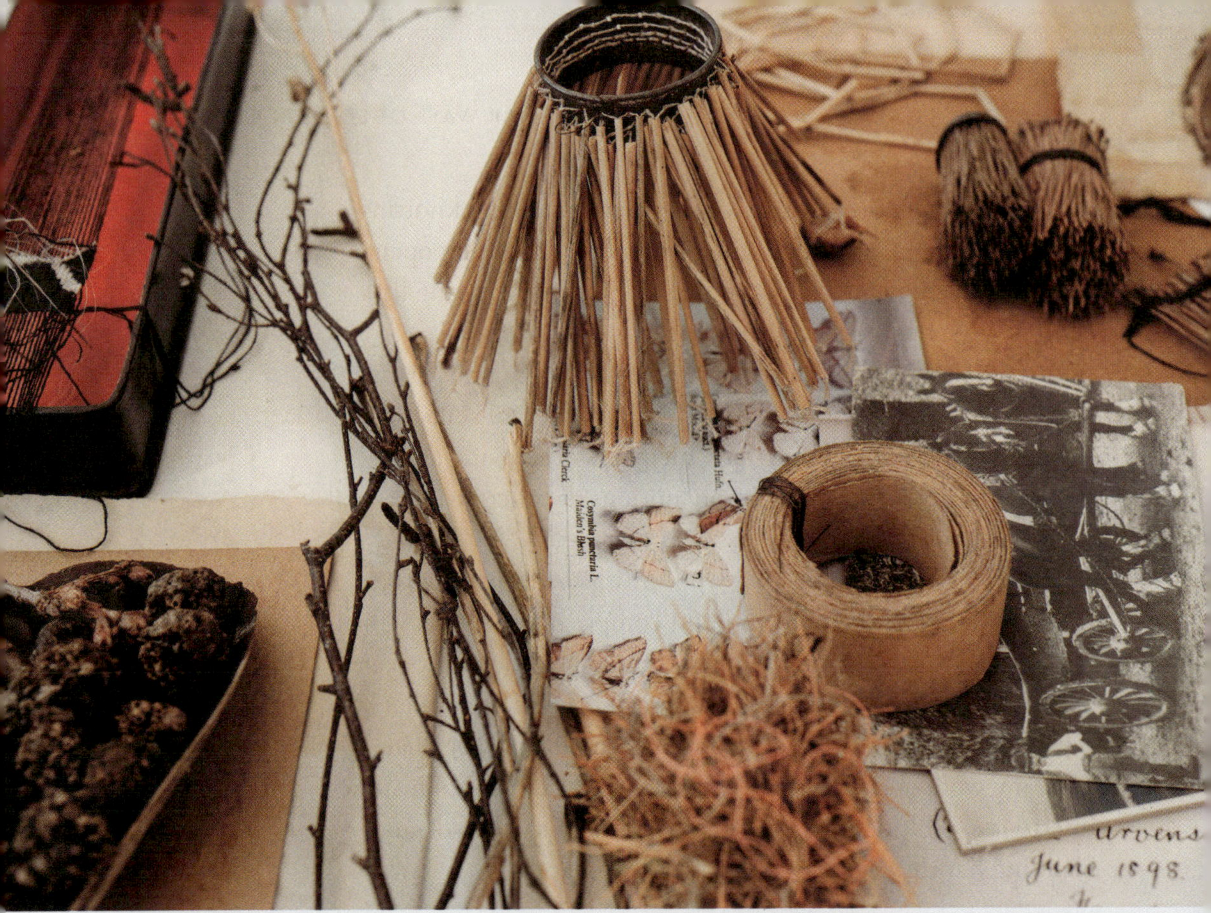

Leaves gathered in my pocket, each holding the memory of an early morning walk, become souvenirs of time spent in nature. Passing through my hands, they are held in care and wonder for their individual beauty. I want to find a way to deepen their narrative, to reveal their story and hidden poetry. Perhaps I'll lay them out in a simple line, giving them space and notice, honouring their quiet significance.

Working intuitively allows me to feel my way into the process of making through curiosity, playfulness, and a series of 'what ifs'. I trust my tacit knowledge as a maker to guide me as I sort, sift, place and order my materials. Handling, observing and arranging is a meditative process that, for me, implies care and mindfulness. So much of the information we take in from our surroundings is subconscious; I have learned how time, memory and place reveal themselves through our fingertips; a sense of corporeal knowledge being communicated by staying with the process, allowing material to be in a state of becoming.

Studio table with tapestry, found objects, pine needles, grass and oak galls. (Photo Esme Mai)

I use slow, repetitive gestures – binding, stitching, knotting and intertwining – setting limitations while remaining open to chance. I enjoy how versatile these skills are, requiring little equipment yet endlessly adaptable.

While I seek simplicity and intuitive ways of making, I also find joy in the contrast of working with traditional skills, many of which are at risk of being lost. Elements of weaving and basketry in my installations imply notions of functionality, rural traditions and social history.

I often leave elements of my work unfinished, inviting the viewer to imagine the maker's hand completing the work which is still open to interpretation and potential. The domestic scale and repurposed nature of my work create a sense of familiarity; these are pieces that feel both common and deeply personal. I hope my work creates a space where personal and social histories intertwine, evoking memories that might otherwise fade and blending nature's marks with the story of place.

Studio table. Crow feathers, grass, daffodil leaves, tin lid, linen threads, archival images. (Photo Jill Walker)

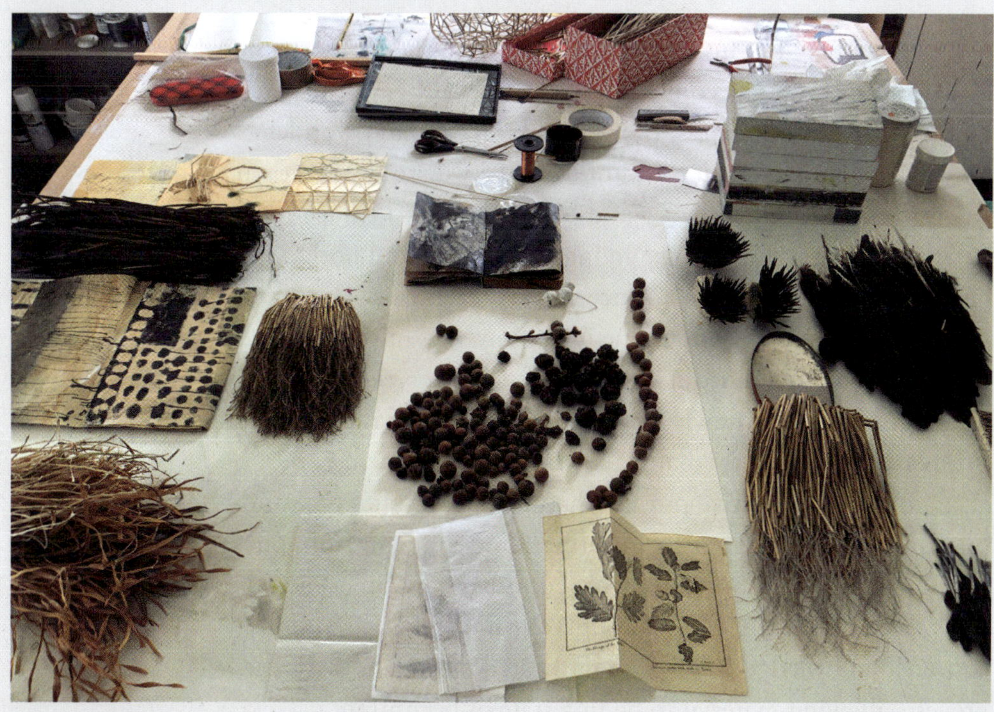

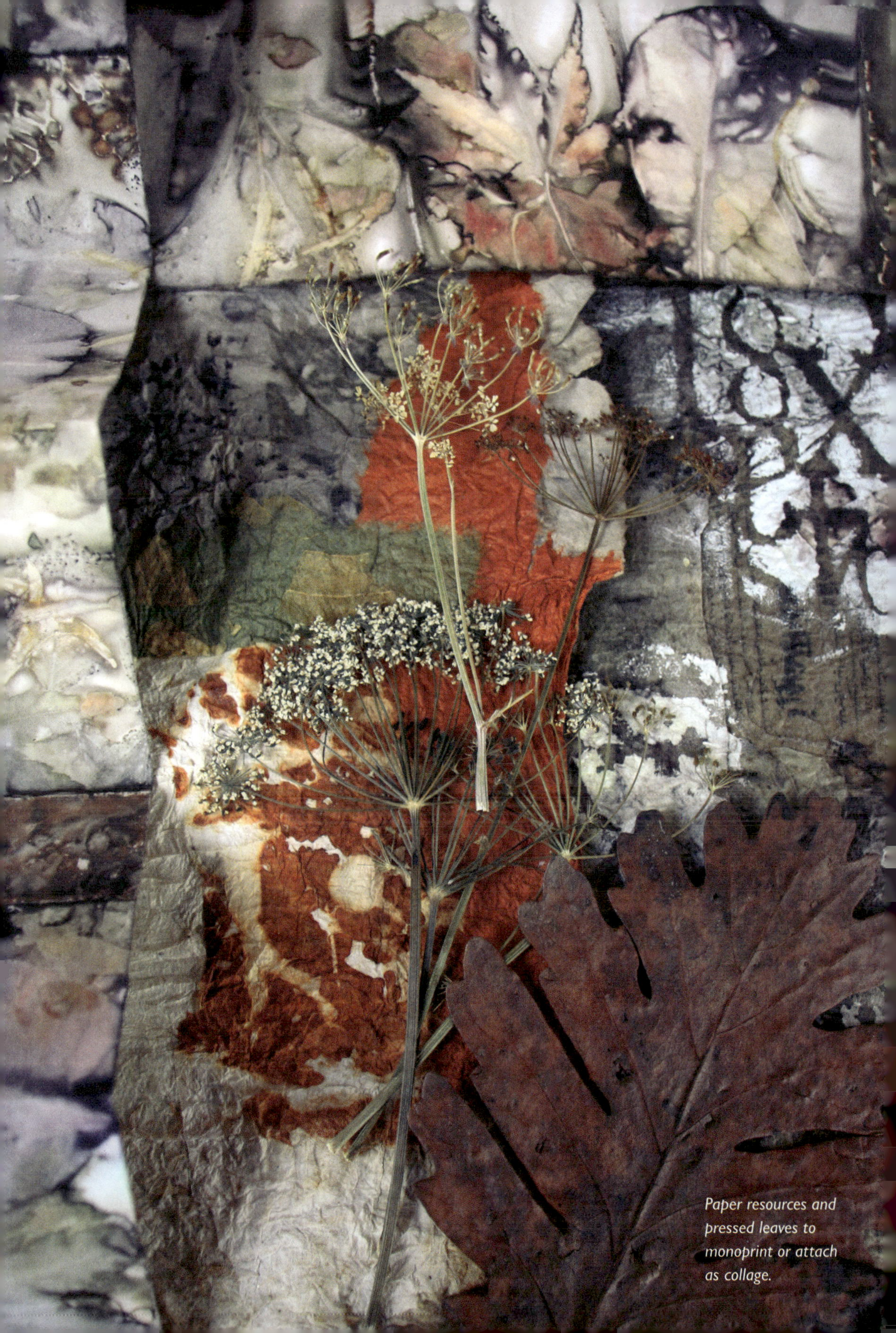

Paper resources and pressed leaves to monoprint or attach as collage.

3

WORKING SEASONALLY: AN ACTIVITY FOR ALL TIMES OF YEAR

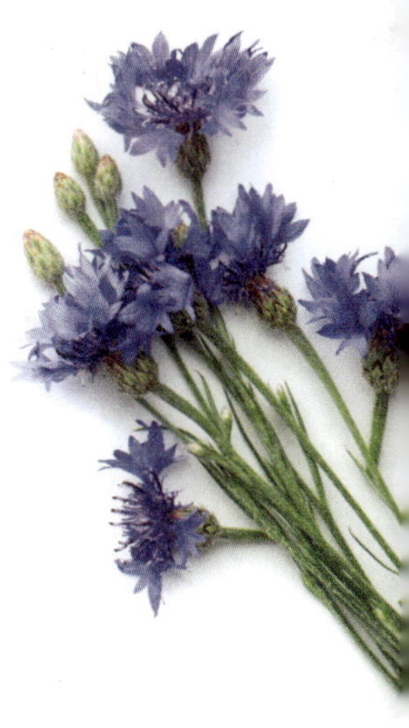

Our hectic, convenient, modern lives often mean that we become detached from the changes the seasons make to the environment so it can be hard to judge when winter, spring, summer and autumn start and finish. As a child, I remember eating certain fresh fruits and vegetables only when they were in season; now we can have strawberries at Christmas and enjoy a kale salad in the summer. Looking at screens as we walk along or working on a laptop on our daily commute, means that we are oblivious to our surroundings. This disconnects us from nature and its seasonal changes and can have a detrimental effect on our mood and wellbeing. Breaking the head down, phone scrolling habit when we're out and about will create the opportunity to look up and outwards; to spot birds in the hedges and plants pushing up through the cracks in the pavements and to notice the impact of the changing seasons on both the rural and urban landscape.

Being aware of the rhythm of the seasons is important if you want to work with natural resources. It helps you choose the best time to gather leaves and plants for botanical contact printing, for example, or when materials can be picked and stored. Working with nature also encourages spontaneity. Some plants bloom only briefly, making the window of opportunity small, while a cyanotype printmaking session relies on summer sunshine, which doesn't always appear as forecast. Having pre-prepared, pre-coated paper stored and ready in a black photographic bag will make it easier to take advantage of an unexpected sunny day.

Some activities are ideal for the winter months when nature is hibernating, the ground is too wet to dig and the weather is not conducive to a long walk. Making sheets of joomchi and collaging with things made and collected during the lighter, brighter months are cheering tasks on a dull winter's day. Working with resources made earlier in the year will bring back memories of warmer times and beautiful places, especially in January and February when the winter feels as though it will never end. Short days and cold, dull weather can lower our spirits and, for some, result in Seasonally Affective Disorder (SAD). Getting out on sunny winter days will help to alleviate some of the symptoms of SAD and creating natural compositions with previously collected material will be distracting and may help to lift a low mood.

Picking Cotinus for botanical contact printing in the summer.

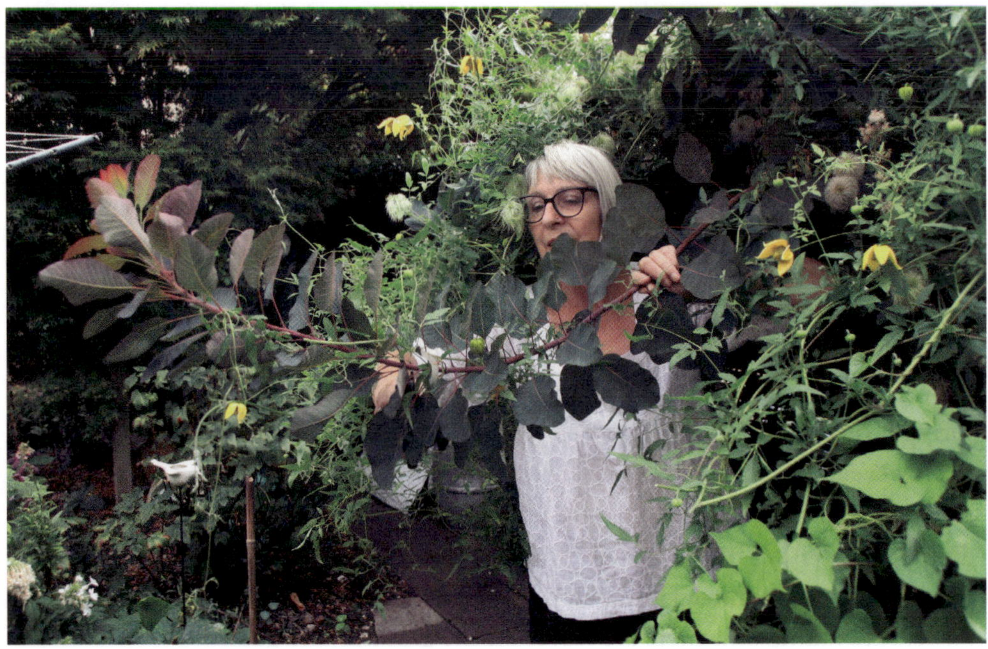

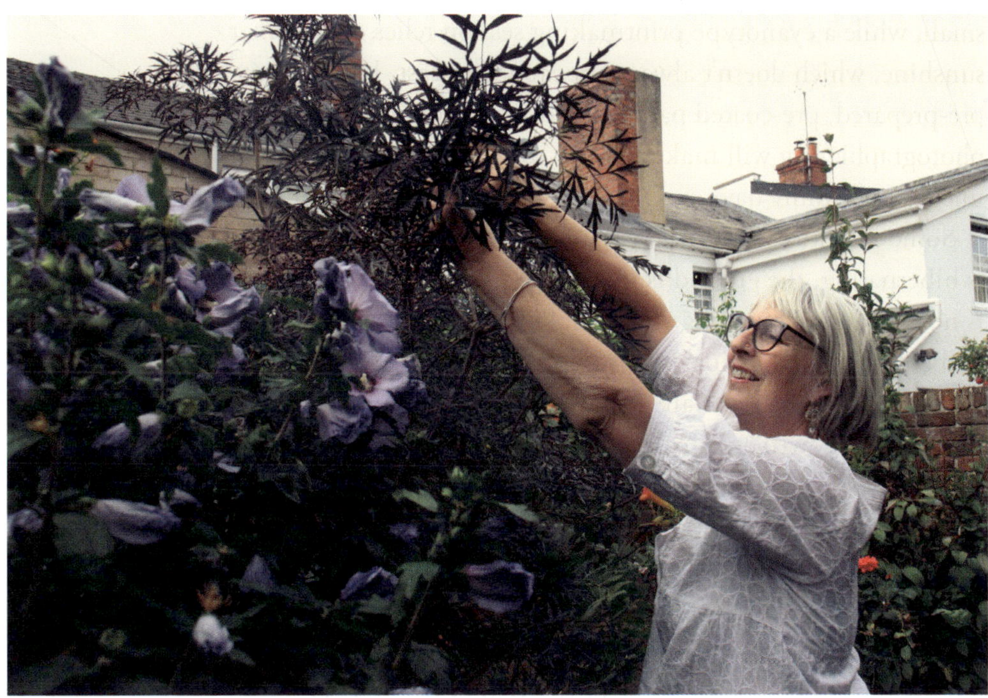

Picking black Elder (sambucus nigra) leaves for botanical contact printing.

Adding collecting and making into a busy working day requires organisation, and perhaps a change in habits. Add a ten-minute lunchtime walk in a local park; stroll around the garden for five minutes when you get back home, even in winter twilight, or make time for an hour's walk once a week. Try to pay attention to your surroundings while you're out – listen for birds, tune in to what's growing around you – as consciously looking and listening is not only restorative but will help to develop an observational practice and a sense of the passing seasons. Other small actions, such as tending a window box or planting spring bulbs, also create a connection with the seasons and, as the bulbs grow and flower, give a clear indication that spring is on its way.

However, opportunities are easily missed. How many of us mean to plant bulbs in the autumn only to find that net full of daffodils sprouting in the shed in December? Life takes over and the snowdrops are missed and before we know it the summer flowers are fading and there are leaves on the ground. The good news is that the seasons will come back round again, nature has a routine that we can tap into at any point; it just takes a bit of planning and preparation to make the most of it. There are tips and hints to collecting and processing those collections for further creative projects throughout this book. Pick one or two of the suggested techniques to begin with, do what is possible in the time available, accept the triumphs and put things that do not go quite to plan to one side; these can always be used as practice pieces at another time.

To avoid missing key points in the seasons, it helps to plan. Making notes in a diary will help keep important seasonal events in the front of your mind. The appearance of hellebores or passion flowers in the garden, for example. Both press well and passion flowers are particularly successful in botanical contact printing, but they bloom only briefly. To avoid missing them, I pop a note in my diary note when I first see them appear and ringfence that time for picking and processing.

Rose leaves are wonderful to press and preseve. Use for monoprinting or botanical contact prints.

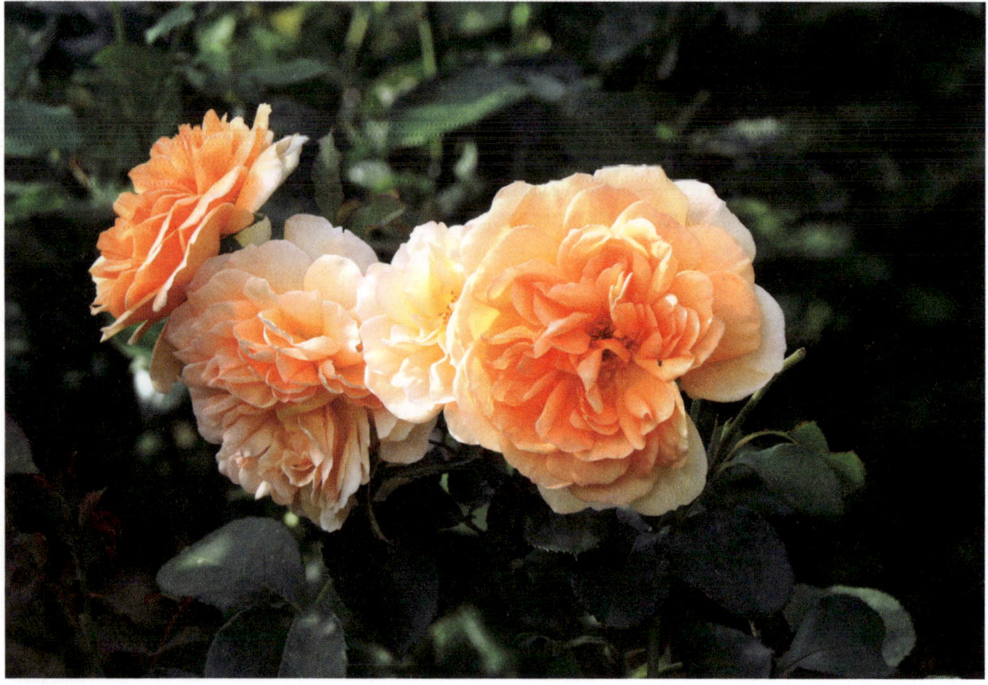

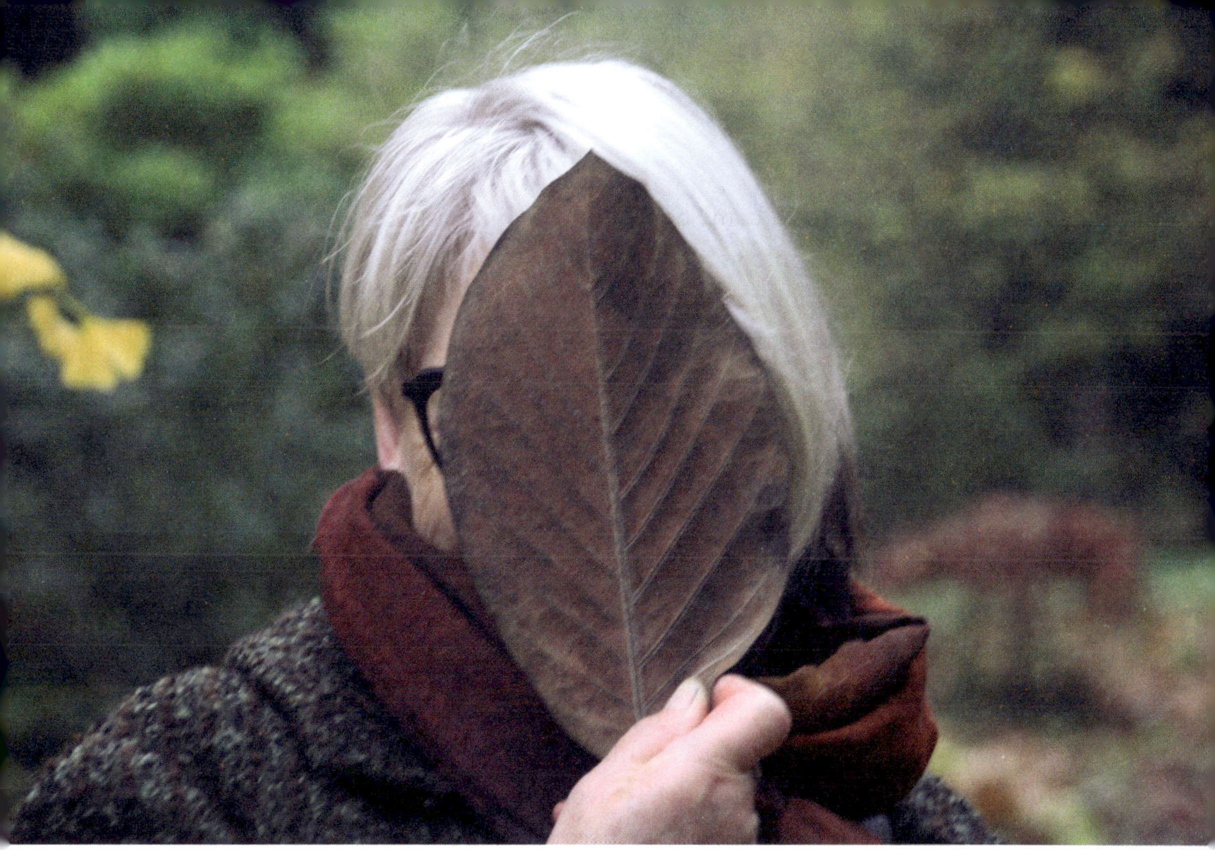

Autumn at Batsford Arboretum.

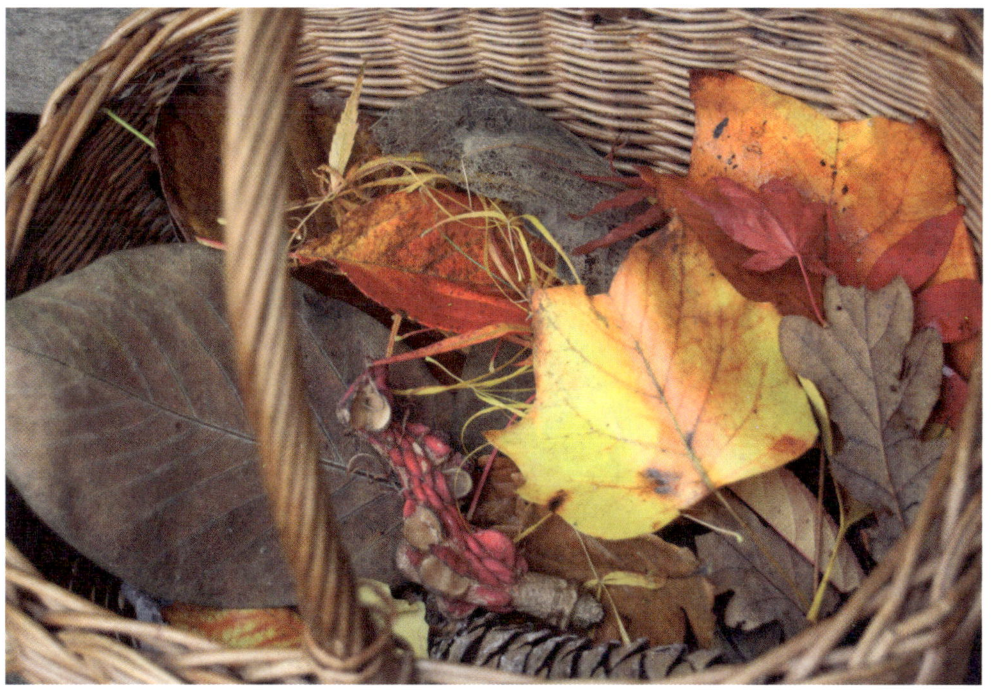

Staggering autumn colour.

A CALENDAR FOR SEASONAL INTENTIONS

Here is a calendar to help plan seasonal activities. You can make notes on it to remind you of the best times for certain collections and plan dates devoted to collecting or making.

	WINTER	SPRING	SUMMER	AUTUMN
JANUARY	Joomchi Natural compositions			
FEBRUARY	Joomchi Natural compositions			
MARCH		Pressing spring flowers		
APRIL		Cyanotype Botanical contact Pressing leaves & flowers		
MAY		Cyanotype Botanical contact Pressing leaves & flowers		
JUNE			Cyanotype Botanical contact Pressing leaves & flowers	
JULY			Cyanotype Botanical contact Pressing leaves & flowers	

	WINTER	SPRING	SUMMER	AUTUMN
AUGUST			Cyanotype Botanical contact Pressing leaves & flowers	
SEPTEMBER			Cyanotype Botanical contact Pressing leaves & flowers	Collecting seed heads
OCTOBER				Collecting seed heads and leaves Monoprinting
NOVEMBER	Joomchi Natural compositions Monoprinting Collecting fallen leaves			Joomchi Natural compositions
DECEMBER	Joomchi Natural compositions Monoprinting			Joomchi Natural compositions Winter sun cyanotypes

PLAN, COLLECT, MAKE

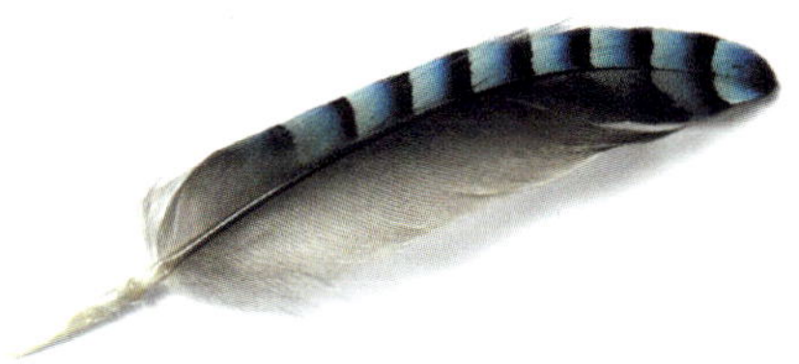

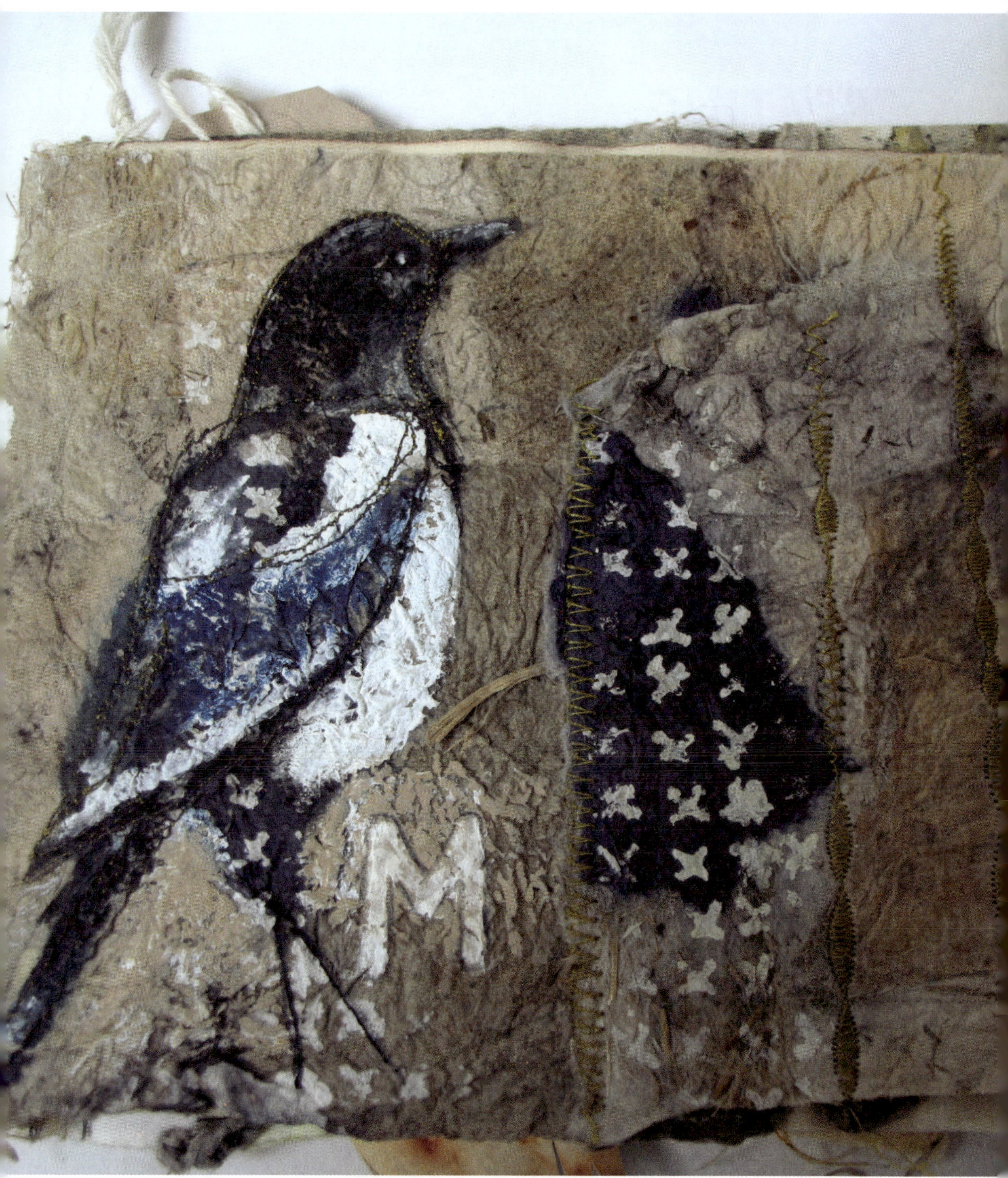

Pages of joomchi stitched into a book form. Collage is added and attached with machine stitching and further embellished with print and paint.

4

CREATING SKETCHBOOKS, JOURNALS AND ARTIST'S BOOKS

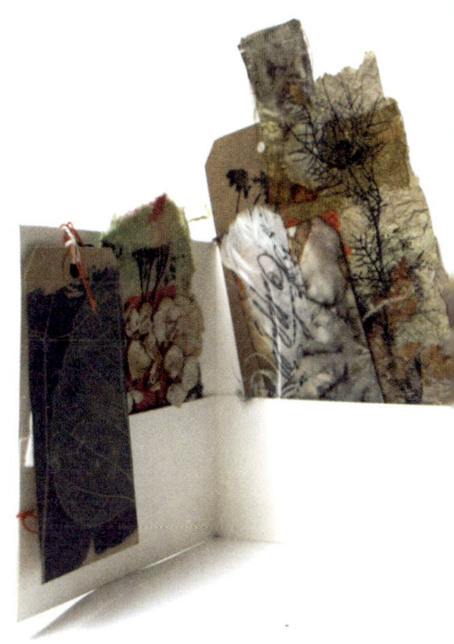

NATURE AND A SKETCHBOOK PRACTICE

Recording nature can take many forms. For some, keeping a diary, journal or sketchbook is part of the routine of their practice. For others, journalling, notating or drawing regularly is an aspiration that never quite gets off the ground. Much like meditating or regular exercise, it's all about making time and creating a habit. It seems so obvious and simple to be told that all one needs is 10 minutes a day to draw something or write down a thought that may turn into an enduring practice. For me just getting over the barrier of getting started is the hardest thing; once I am working in my sketchbook, time flies but opening that book is the tough part.

Another barrier to creating a regular sketchbook or diary practice is knowing what to put into it. That empty first page is daunting; a new journal or sketchbook is so fresh and unspoilt but remember, it's just sheets of paper and the book is for your eyes only. You could use it to date a collection and record the location of the various leaves and flowers, or to note what works best for various effects – all information that can be used in future projects. Or you could use the pages to explore your aesthetic by collaging papers and monoprinting directly into the book. The pile of joomchi, botanical printed and monoprinted papers and cyanotypes that have built up as you have worked through the techniques in these pages could be a good place to begin.

Here are a few guidelines that might make it easier to start a regular – or even an irregular – sketchbook or journal practice using nature as a starting point.

- Start with a spot of shopping and buy a book that will be enticing to work in. This might be a notebook with an appealing cover or a hardback sketchbook. A fancy stationary shop, art suppliers or even a charity shop can offer a book that will feel encouraging. It is useful to have a sketchbook that has a minimum of 170gm paper to take a variety of media but thinner papers will work too, just be aware these pages may wrinkle when glued or painted.

Sketch books using paper made from natural resources.

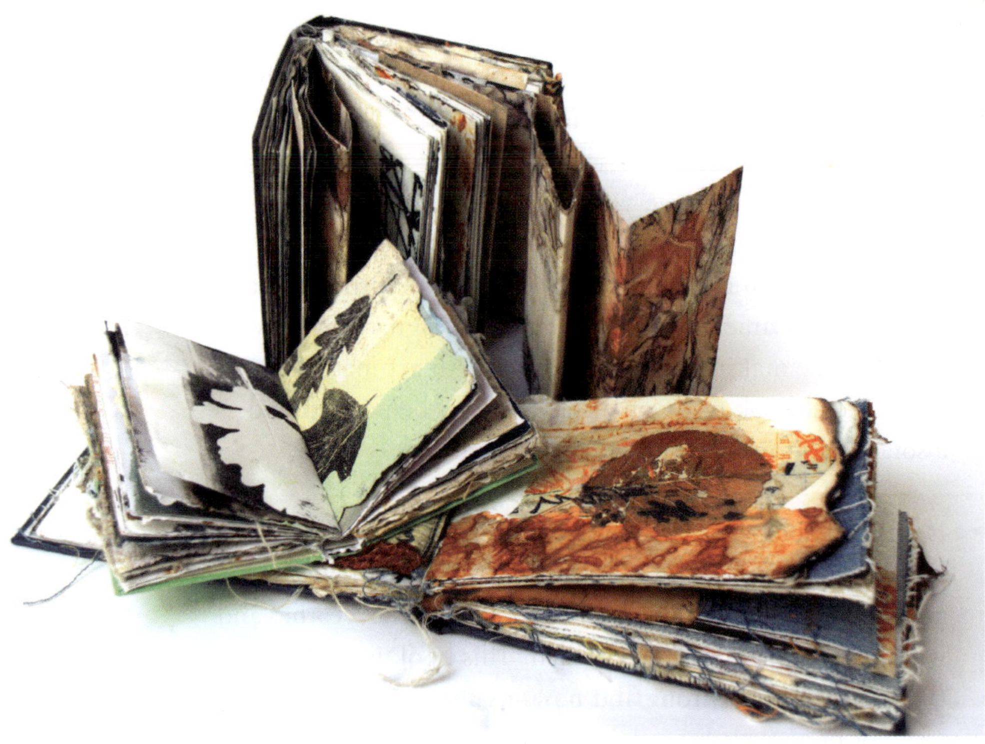

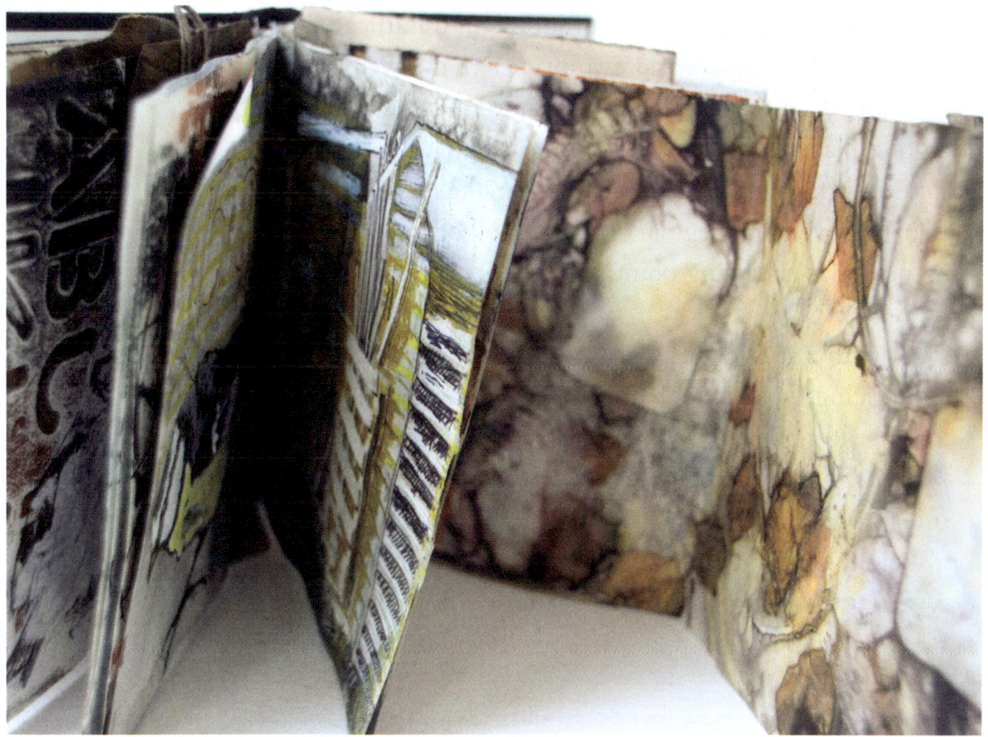

- For a regular sketchbook practice, use a small A5 sized book – anything larger can feel daunting.

A commercial sketchbook with an added page of botanical contact paper.

- Create an area where everything you need to write, draw or stick into the book is to hand – having to look for everything when the creative mood strikes is distracting and uses precious time. Not everyone has a designated creative space, so try making a mobile station with art materials and a sketchbook ready on a tray that can be popped under a sofa, bed or in a cupboard when not in use.

- It's not all about drawing a masterpiece. Part of a daily practice might be sticking down some collage, drawing around collected leaves or making a note of the weather and what has popped up in the garden. This book is for you so there's no right or wrong and no 'musts' or 'shoulds'. Draw, write or press flowers in it; it is a personal choice.

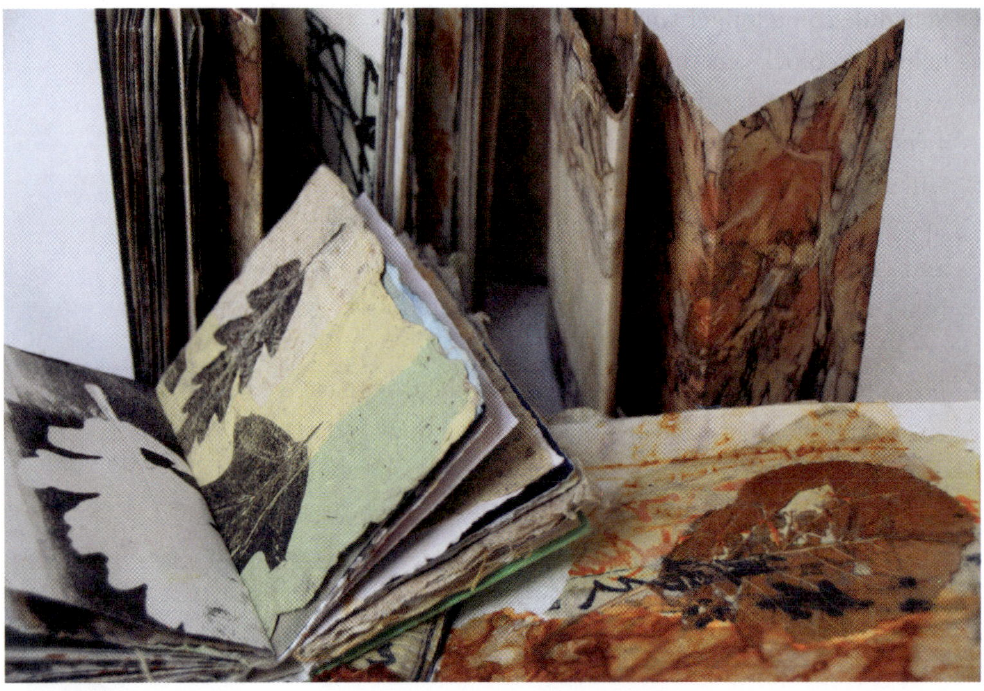

Pages using monoprints, botanical contact paper and stitched pressed leaves.

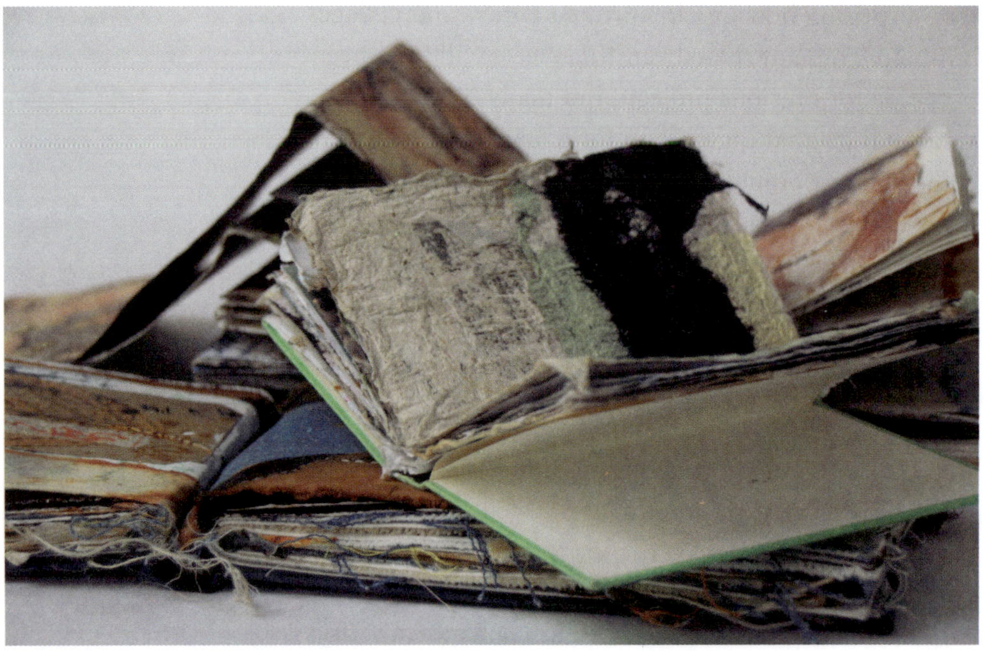

Handmade books using joomchi.

- Schedule some longer time to work in the book. It can be helpful to block out time in a diary. Using the rule about working for longer than it takes to set up and clear away a chosen activity means a technique can be selected that will not leave you feeling rushed or chaotic when tidying up. A morning might allow time to experiment with collage and drawing. A longer period will make it worth getting out inks and monoprinting directly into a sketchbook.

- It can be daunting to start a new book at the front page – somehow the first page of a pristine sketchbook is nerve wracking and, if the book has no dates (in which case it makes sense for pages to follow on consecutively), it can be easier to start in the middle. Hiding that first tentative entry deep inside will leave the first page free for a more confident entry.

MAKING ARTIST'S BOOKS

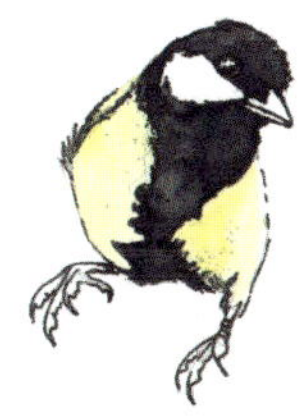

It is surprising how quickly printed papers and collages build up. Some of these beautiful sheets will have been put aside for precious projects and many others cut, stuck and printed together to form aesthetically pleasing compositions. Some of these creations may be destined to be framed and admired, or given as bespoke cards to special friends who appreciate handmade presents. Spending a day or so on any of the techniques in this book will produce a mass of creative resources for you to develop further. Using some of them to make artist's books is a useful way of focusing on a beautiful collection, as well as storing and displaying treasured compositions.

An artist's book is a work of art created in the form of a book where the book itself becomes the artwork, rather than simply a vehicle for display. The focus is on the book's structure, material and how it interacts with its content. An artist's book often challenges conventional notions of what a book can be.

Artist's books do not need to be complicated or involve intricate sewing techniques. Here are a few suggestions for ways to use the piles of natural resources you have made. But be warned, these simple ideas may well lead you to explore more complicated book forms!

Concertina and slit books

Some botanical contact paper and joomchi are just too nice to cut up for collage, but it's a shame to leave them languishing in a folder where they will only make your heart sing when you come across them accidently while searching for something else, or tidying your studio. Folding these treasures into a concertina or slit book is an effective way of allowing them to be displayed and handled. Folding paper into a form that will stand upright gives it physical integrity that a single, unformed sheet of paper lacks.

A very simple concertina book.

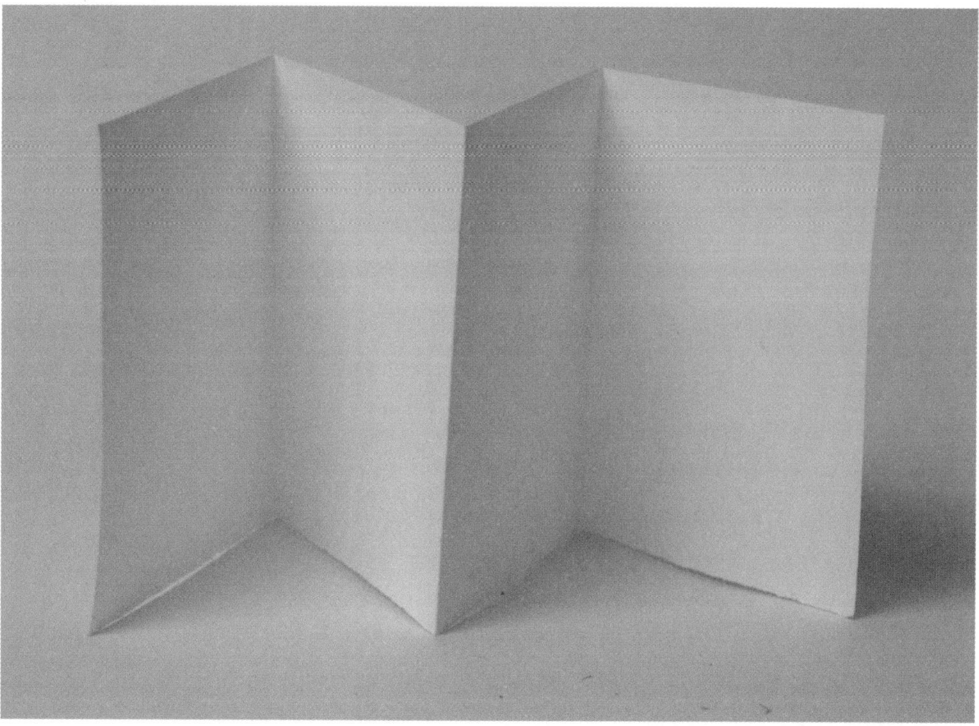

Botanical contact paper folded into a concertina book. Further printing and mixed media collage has been added.

Delicate paper can be botanical contact printed and folded into a book.

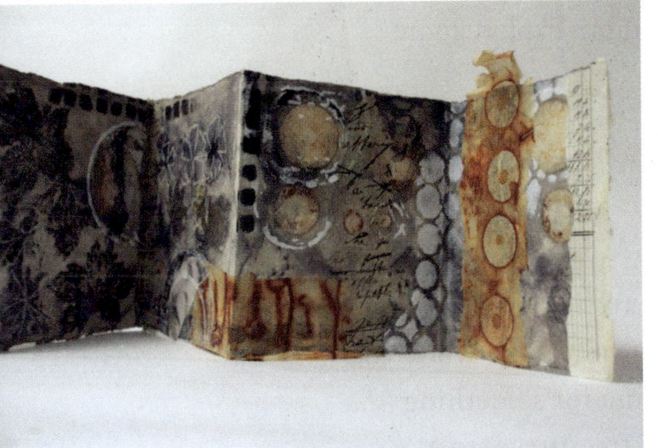

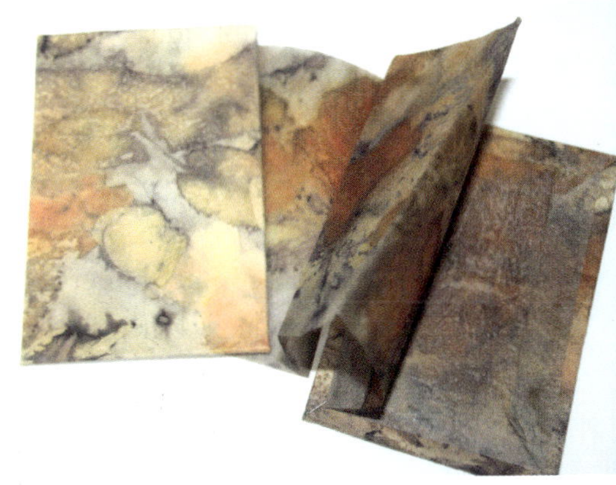

Concertina book

A concertina is one of the simplest book forms, requiring little in the way of measuring and cutting. And it is an effective way to use that large sheet of prized botanical contact printed paper that's just too successful to cut up. However, while this is a simple form, it is worth practicing with a plain piece of paper first.

Equipment

- Cutting board
- Craft knife with a new blade
- Steel safety ruler
- Paper folder or butter knife

Materials

- Various papers
- Glue

1. Cut, or rip along the edge of a steel ruler, a piece of paper measuring 42cm x 14cm (16½ x 5½in).

2. Take the paper and fold in half, short end to short end.

3. Using the edge of a paper folder or butter knife, press in the crease.

4. Fold both short ends to the centre fold, creating four pages. Again, reinforce the folds. This is now a four page concertina book.

5. To create eight pages, continue to fold edge to fold and folded edge to folded edge, reinforcing the folds at each stage with a paper folder or butter knife.

6. Look at the book form to check that the folds are alternating in and out to create a concertina. This may mean reversing one or two folds to make it zig zag evenly.

Delicious botanical contact paper folded into concertina book forms.

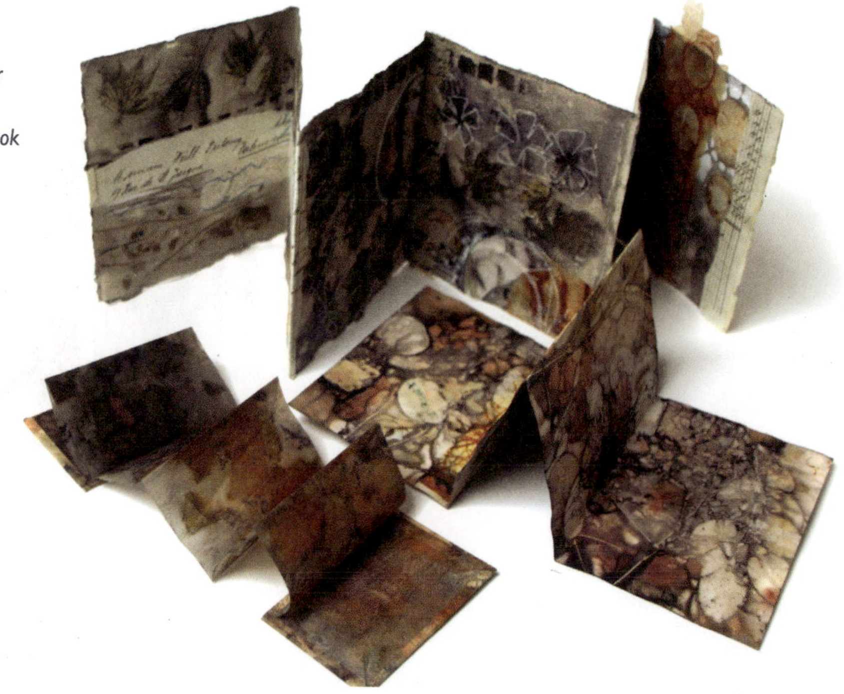

Extensions

- To make a longer book, add another concertina of the same size by taping the back edge of the first book to the front edge of the next book.

- Use the concertina book as a sketchbook or journal, adding observations or sticking in collected leaves and flowers.

- Ideally, a concertina needs to be made from firm paper. However, delicate books can be made with botanical contact paper printed onto tissues. These thin books will not stand up, but the results can be pleasing.

Slit books

Also known as zines or pamphlet books, this book form creates a recognisable four-page booklet. Don't worry too much about the edges meeting and being even, especially when using joomchi: the more rustic-looking the better. If you do not have a large enough piece of joomchi, glue a couple of pieces together to make the folding easier.

1. Fold the paper in half, long edge to long edge, and press the crease in with a paper folder or butter knife

2. Unfold, then refold the paper again in half, short end to short end. Press the crease in.

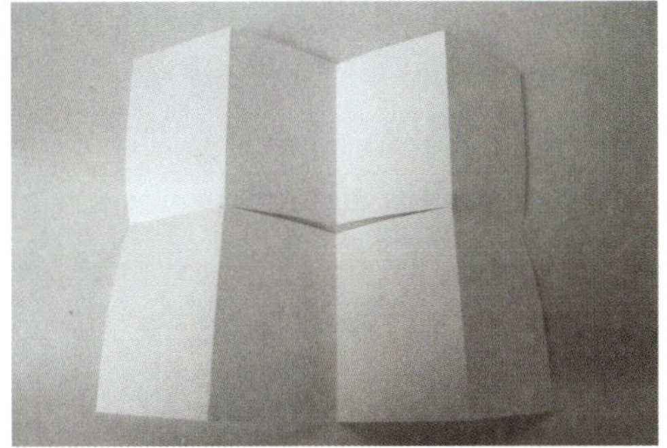

The folds and cut for a slit book.

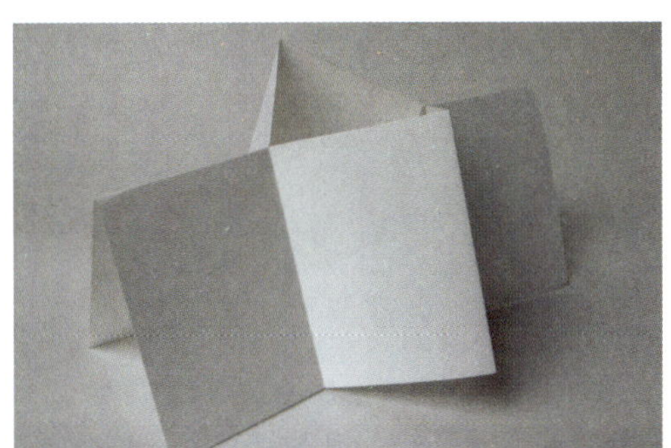

Constructing a slit book.

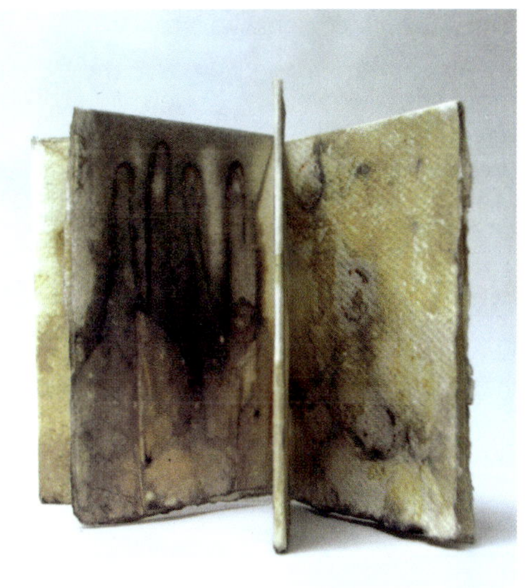

A slit book completed as a 4-page leaflet.

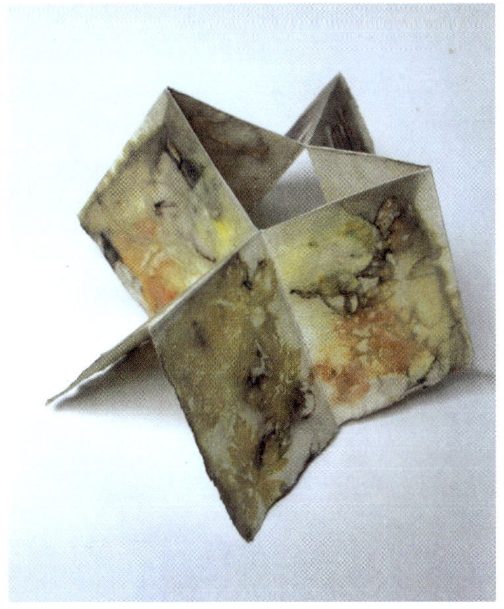

Botanical contact paper made into a slit book.

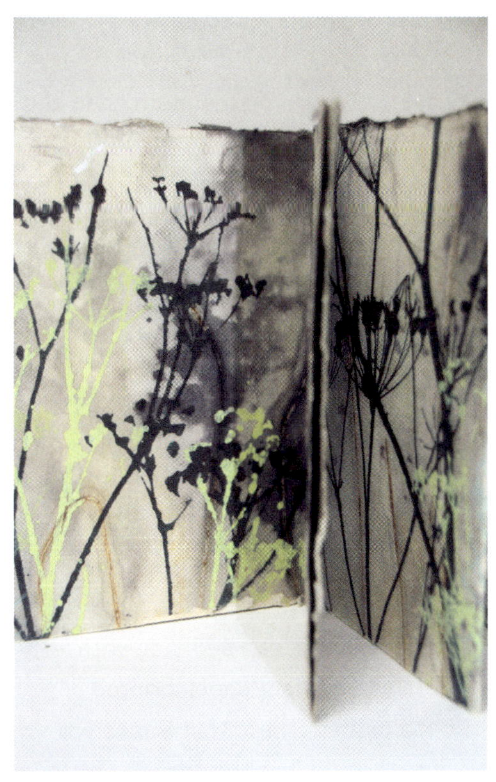

Monoprinting directly into the pages of a slit book.

3 Fold each edge back to the fold on either side and reinforce the crease.

4 Open out the paper and mark the middle crease.

5 Cut the middle crease with a craft knife against a ruler.

6 Stand up the half-folded paper and pull out the centre creases to form middle and end pages.

7 Push the pages into a four-page booklet.

Extensions

* Joomchi lends itself to stitching and this book will benefit from having the pages stitched in place. Both hand and machine stitching will work on this fibre-like paper.

* Glue the edges together to create a firmer book.

* Turn the book upside down and use the open ends as collecting pockets. (See Slit book with pockets below) This may require gluing some of the sides together so that collected items do not fall out.

Slit book with pockets

A useful extension to the slit book form is to add pockets. These make the book ideal for taking on collecting walks or keeping small collages and precious finds together.

* Create a four-page slit book, making the pages 14cm (5½in) high. Extend the slit to one edge of the paper, creating a hinge.

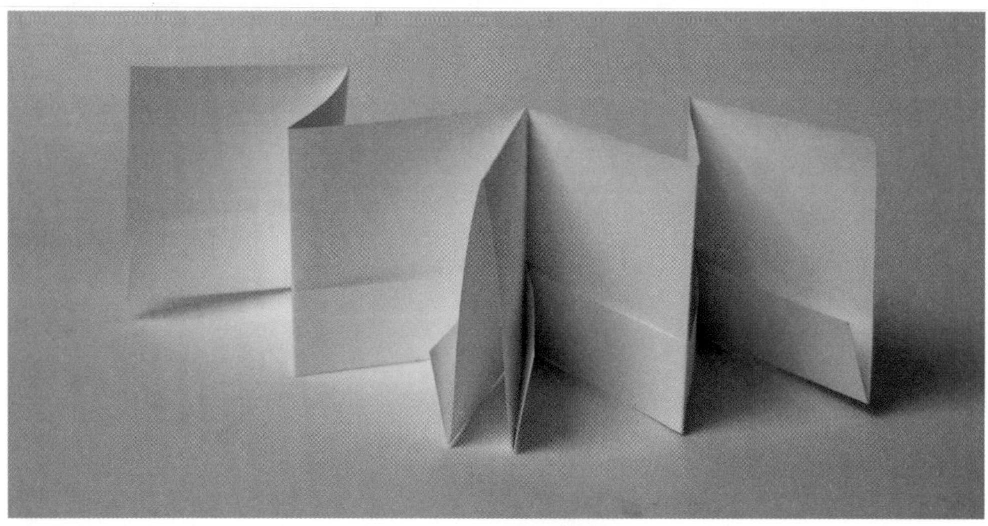

Slit book with pockets.

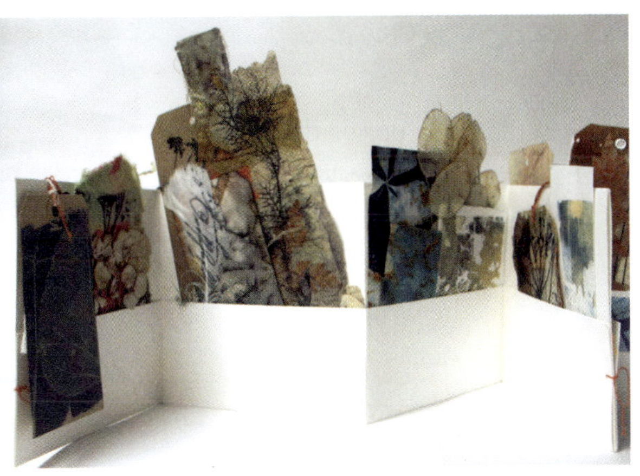 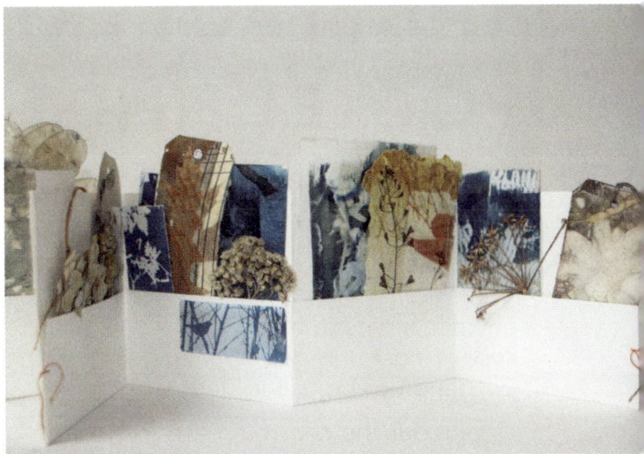

A concertina pocket book is ideal to display collections and snippets of collage.

- Measure 4cm (1½in) along both long edges and score a line from end to end against a ruler using the paper folder. This will form the pocket.

- Fold the 4cm (1½in) width away from the line and reinforce the fold with a paper folder.

- Gently re-fold the book form, including the 4cm (1½in) width, to create a pocket for each page.

- Glue, or put a single stitch, at each end of the open pocket sections so that collections will not fall out.

- When making this book the folds will be more preciseif you use a thin cartridge paper. Thicker papers make less precise folds resulting in a more organic, natural book form.

Further experiments

Experiment with the scale of these books. Create larger sheets of paper by gluing or stitching them together. The bigger the paper, the larger the book.

Do not be hampered by accuracy – unless that is the required outcome. It takes practice to measure and cut accurately and there is a charm to a book that has a hand made look to it.

CUT, STICK, FOLD

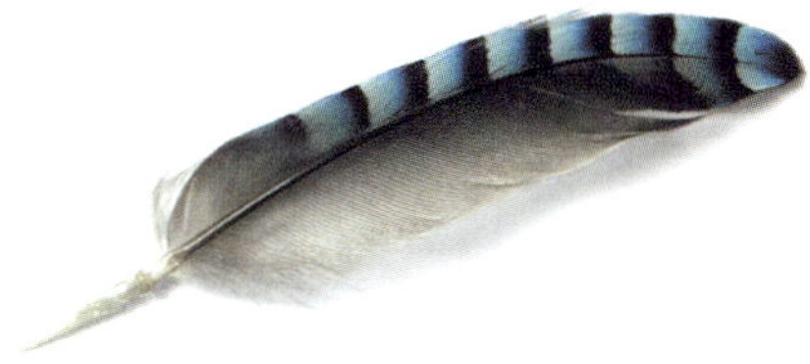

THE BEAUTY OF THE POCKET FIND

TARA AXFORD

Tara Axford is a mixed media artist from Sydney, Australia, working in prints, collage, fibre arts and photography. Inspired by her surroundings, she seeks patterns, textures and imperfections, focusing on forgotten, or weathered objects. She photographs and arranges found elements to highlight overlooked details, abstracting environments so viewers see them with a new perspective.

There is a quiet kind of magic in the act of noticing. Years ago while on holiday in Europe, I watched a woman crouch in the grounds of a sixteenth-century castle to pick up what looked like a fallen leaf. She tucked it into her coat pocket and kept walking. I smiled to myself and thought, 'Ah, she's one of us.' Since then, I've come to realise how many people quietly, instinctively, engage in the same ritual, gathering natural bits and bobs on walks, creating miniature collections; each piece a gentle reminder or souvenir of a place visited.

My practice revolves around these 'pocket finds.' It is a process of discovery, a response to place and a way of translating the essence of a moment into something tangible, but not always permanent. I am less concerned with preserving these objects in a fixed form and than in discovering what they stir within me creatively. The act of finding, handling, arranging – it all becomes part of the story.

Originally trained as a graphic designer and art director, spending many years balancing a creative career with family life and learned to work in 'pockets of time'; those little in-between spaces where creativity can flourish without needing to be a grand event. This mindset naturally extended to my growing fascination with collections from nature. A humble leaf, a rusted washer, a feather on a footpath, something found and saved could spark something new.

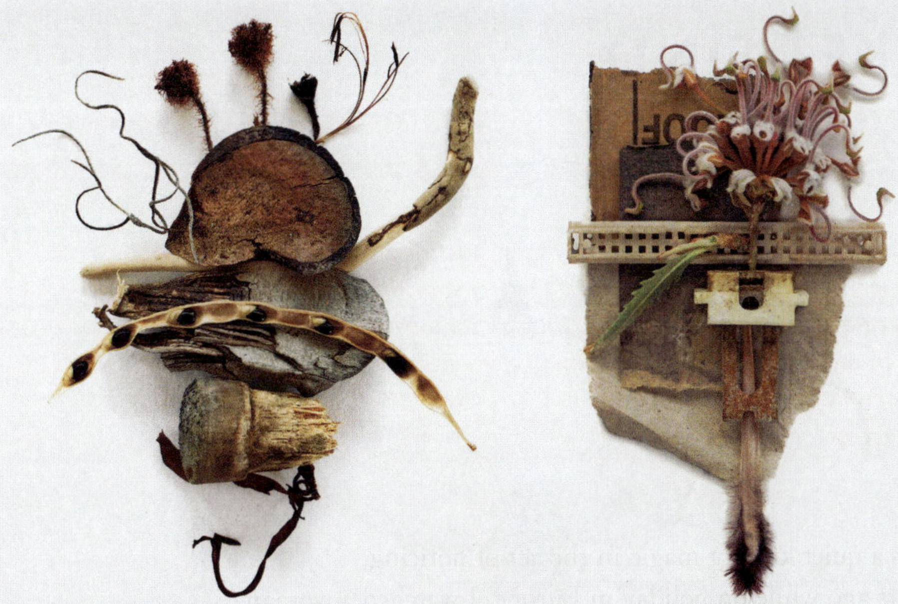

Pocket find arrangements by Tara Axford.

My artistic process is rooted in response, not replication. I'm not trying to render nature realistically; my camera already does that. Instead, I want to distil a place into colour, texture and form. My studio is filled with segmented drawers and boxes: sea glass, seed pods, sun-bleached bone fragments. Each collection is a visual vocabulary I return to. These finds offer me a way to 'see with my hands.'

What is fascinating is that a walk with no creative agenda often yields the most inspiring materials. I let instinct lead. Sometimes I set a small challenge: 'collect only five pieces', and find that limitation might fuel focus. Once home, I begin sorting by colour or shape. This tactile, meditative stage often leads to ephemeral compositions, photographed on simple white paper and captured before a petal curls or a leaf wilts.

The beauty of this practice is its accessibility. No specialist tools are required. Just a pocket (or small bag), a curious mind and a willingness to notice. It's a way of slowing down, of connecting with our surroundings and, perhaps, with ourselves.

During the pandemic, my world, like many others', became smaller. My neighbourhood walks, those well-trodden loops, transformed into treasure hunts. I began to recognise where particular plants grew and what changed with the seasons. What had once felt ordinary became a source of creative renewal.

Pocket find arrangements by Tara Axford.

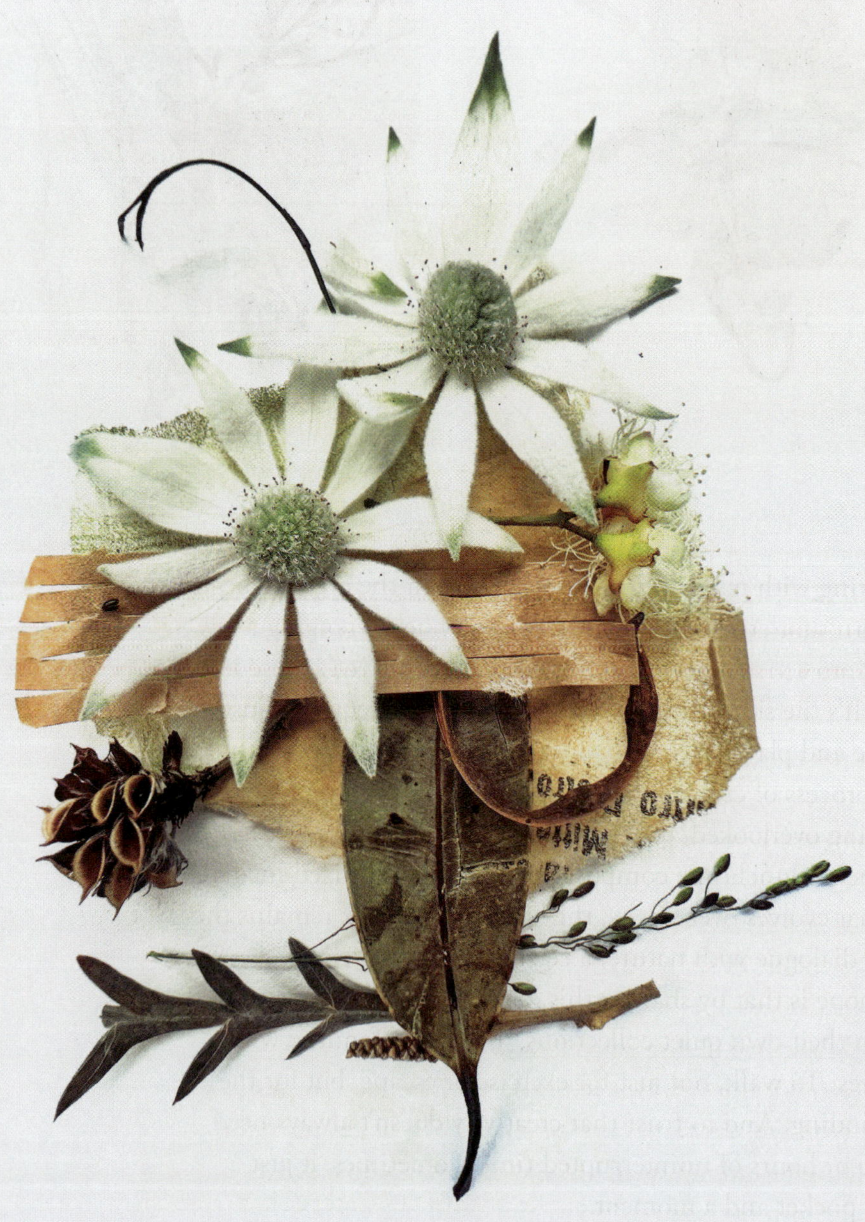

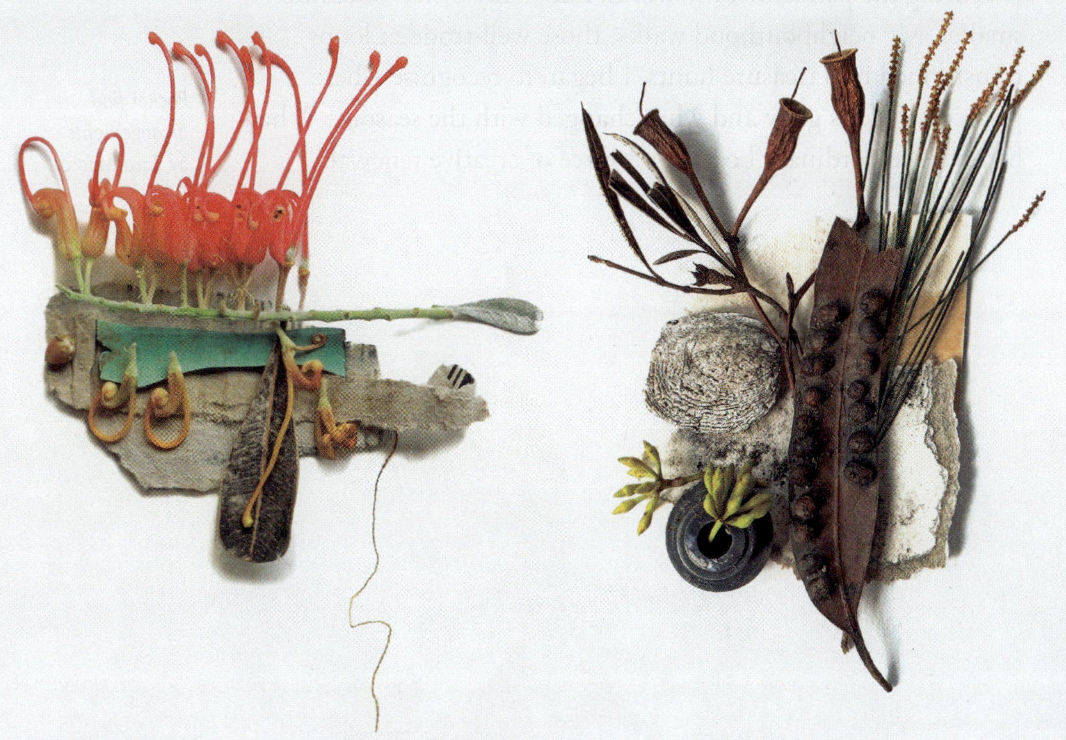

Working with natural finds also helps train the eye. We begin
to discern subtleties in shape, pattern and hue. Arranging a few
objects into a visual harmony becomes an intuitive exercise in
design. It's the simplest kind of collage, no glue required, just
presence and play.

The process of creating something from nothing, or from
something overlooked, continues to thrill me. Whether it's a
spontaneous lunchtime composition or a layered mixed-media
piece that evolves over weeks, the heart of the work remains the
same: a dialogue with nature, a celebration of noticing.

My hope is that by sharing this, others might be inspired
to begin their own quiet collections. To see the familiar with
fresh eyes. To walk, not just for exercise or escape, but for the
joy of finding. And to trust that creativity doesn't always need
a studio or hours of uninterrupted time. Sometimes, it just
needs a pocket and a moment.

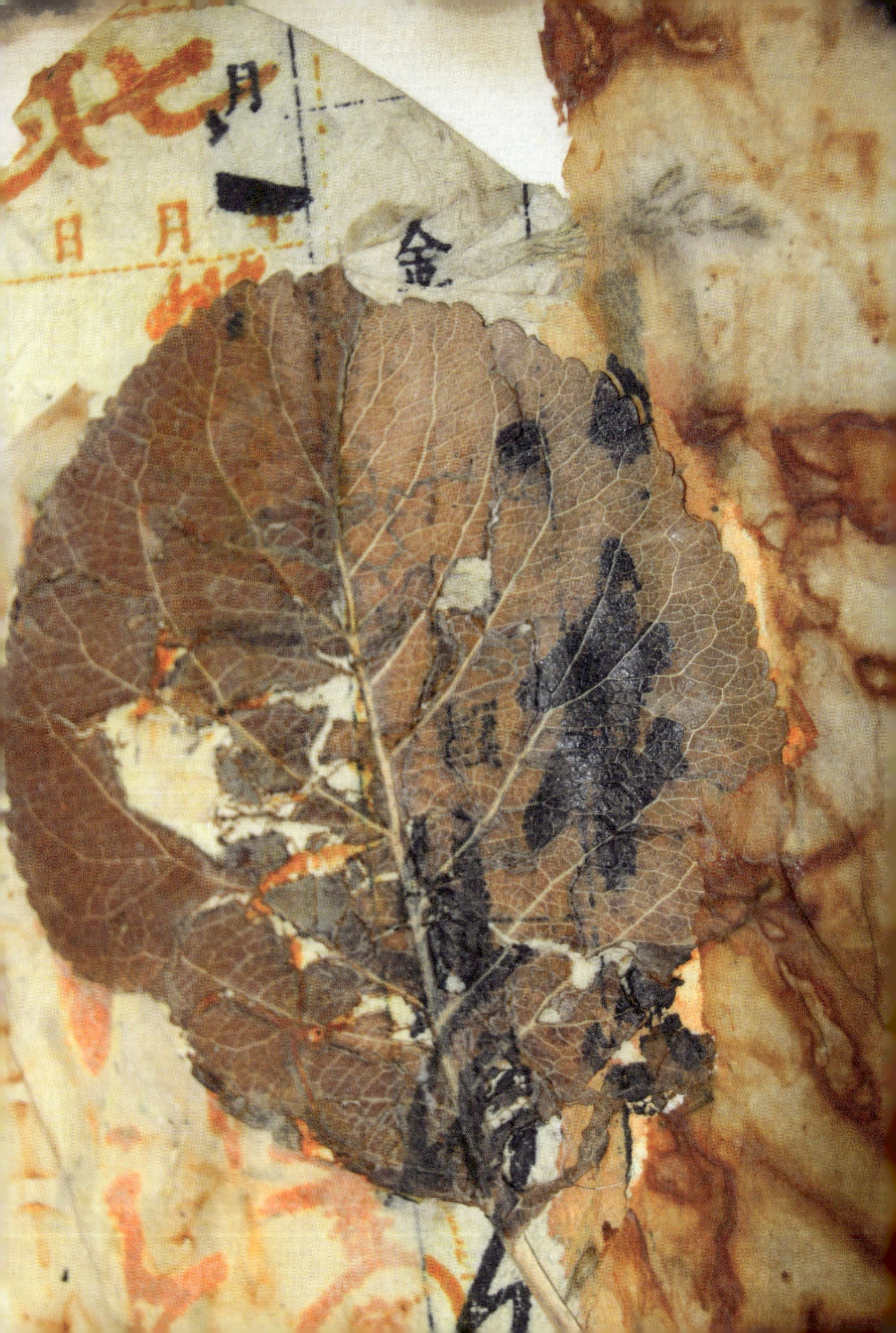
七月
月
日 月
金
日

FINALLY

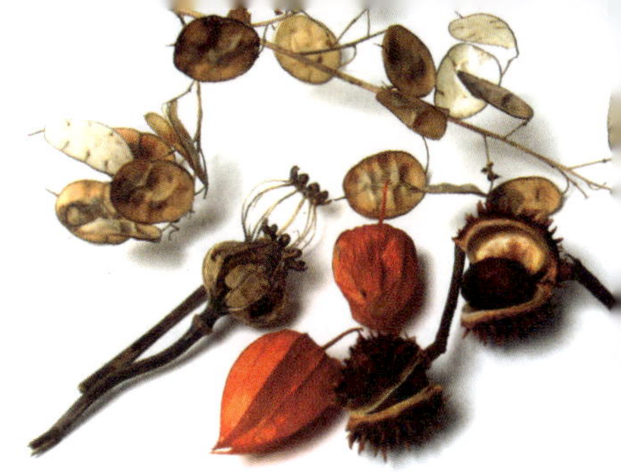

As I sit writing this in my garden studio at the end of July, I am distracted by the birds calling, a large dragon fly whizzing past the door and a gentle breeze moving the plants in my dishevelled, overgrown garden. The sun is out so I am itching to make some cyanotypes, to pick passion flowers for pressing and printing later and to use my abundant Sambuca for a botanical print before it gets its autumn prune. I am not thinking about what art I can make with these techniques; that is for the future. Simply setting these intentions makes me feel connected to the world outside.

My aim in writing *Collect, Print, Collage* is to share some of the techniques I use and my enthusiasm to combine them to create seasonally-inspired records of my urban garden and a creative response to my natural environment. For you as a reader, it may generate ideas to try later as the seasons come around. Or perhaps it will suggest a process that will add another dimension to a planned project, or a technique that could be a starting point for a new one.

However you choose to use it, I hope *Collect, Print, Collage* offers a connection to creating seasonally and with the flow of the natural world. I hope too that it provides the inspiration to slow and calm busy lives through looking at the changes around us and recording them in a gentle and mindful way.

COLLECT, PRINT, COLLAGE

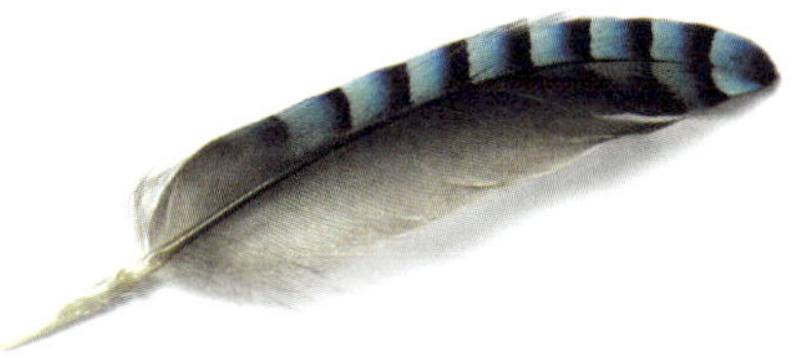

SUPPLIERS

UK

Hawthorn Printmaker Supplies

The Workshop, York. YO19 5UH
www.hawthornprintmaker.com

For inks and equipment.
Ink, rollers and presses.

Handprinted

22 Arun Business Park, Shripney Road,
Bognor Regis PO22 9SX
www.handprinted.co.uk

Specialist printmaking supplies. General
art sundries for mixed media on paper and
textiles. Cyanotype kits, rollers, papers and
sketchbooks.

Intaglio Printmaker

9 Playhouse Court, 62 Southwark Bridge
Road, London SE1 0AT
www.intaglioprintmaker.com

Specialist printmaking suppliers of paper, inks
and rollers.

John Purcell Paper

15 Rumsey Road, London SW9 0TR
www.johnpurcell.net

Paper suppliers

Great Art

41-49 Kingsland Road,
London E2 8AG
www.greatart.co.uk

General art suppliers of paper, paint
and inks and some printmaking supplies

Jacksons Art Supplies

1 Farleigh Place, London N16 7SX
www.jacksonsart.com

General art supplies including some
printmaking inks and sundries

Seawhite of Brighton

Star Road Trading Estate,
West Sussex RH13 8RY
www.seawhite.co.uk

Sketchbook and paper suppliers

USA

Takach Press

2815 Broadway S.E. Albuquerque NM 87102
https://shop.takachpress.com/

Printmaking supplies.

Dick Blick Art Materials

P.O. Box 1267 Galesburg, IL 61402-1267
www.dickblick.com

Printmaking supplies and general art sundries.

Graphic Chemical

728 North Yale Avenue, Villa Park. IL 60181
www.graphicchemical.com

Printmaking suppliers.

Utrecht Art Supplies

PO Box 1267, Galesburg, IL 61402-1267
www.utrechtart.com

Printmaking supplies and general art sundries.

FURTHER READING

I have tried to introduce a variety of techniques to you in this book, just scratching the surface of the possibilities of each process. This might whet your appetite to dive deeper into a technique. There is so much information online that it can become overwhelming and difficult to know where to start. Here I have listed a few books for future reading. These publications may sign post you towards processes in more detail and suggest other ways of developing projects. I prefer to curl up with a book or have the inspirational page open while I work as an antidote to looking at a screen for information (although an interesting artist on Instagram can be very inspiring too).

Here are a few of my favourite resource books offering inspirational and further technical details.

Creativity through Nature: Foraged, Recycled and Natural Mixed-Media Art, Ann Blockley, Batsford. ISBN 978-1-84994-649-0

Paper Lithography, Sue Brown, The Crowood Press, 2023. ISBN 978-0-7198-4205-4

Creative Cyanotype: Techniques and Inspiration, Angela Chalmers, The Crowood Press, 2023. ISBN 978-0-7198-4267-2

Bound: Over 20 Artful Handmade Books, Erica Ekrem, Lark, 2015. ISBN 978-1-4547-0867-4

Eco Colour: Botanical dyes for beautiful textiles, India Flint, Murdoch Books, 2021. ISBN 978-1741960792

Natural Processes in Textile Art: From Rust Dyeing to Found Objects, Alice Fox, Batsford, 2015. ISBN 978-1-84994-298-0

Bound: 15 beautiful bookbinding projects, Rachel Hazell, Kyle Books, 2018. ISBN 978-0-85783-507-9

The Art of the Fold: How to Make Innovative Books and Paper Structures, Hedi Kyle and Ulla Warchol, Laurence King Publishing, 2018. ISBN 978-1-78627-293-5

Poetic Cloth: Creating meaning in textile art, Hannah Lamb, Batsford, 2019. IBSN 978-1-84994-536-3

Make Ink: A Forager's Guide to Natural Inkmaking, Jason Logan, Abrams, 2018. ISBN 978-1-4197-3243-0

The Organic Artist: Make Your Own Paint, Paper, Pigments, Prints and More from Nature, Nick Neddo, Quarry Books, 2015. ISBN 978-1-59253-926-0

Sketchbook Explorations for Mixed-media and Textile Artists, Shelley Rhodes, Batsford, 2018. ISBN 978-84994-480-9

Book + Art: Handcrafting Artists' Books, Dorothy Simpson Krause. North Light Books, 2009. ISBN 978-1-60061-154-4

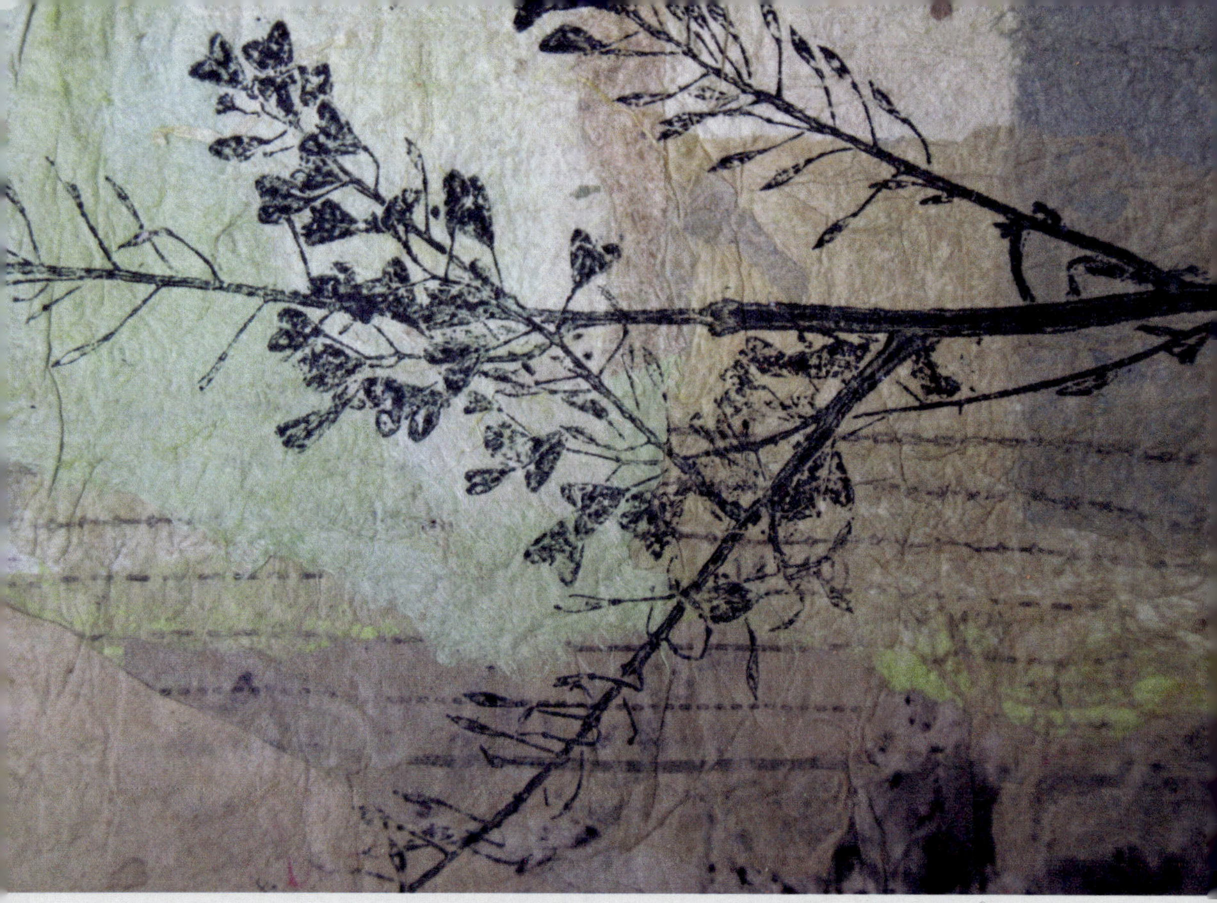

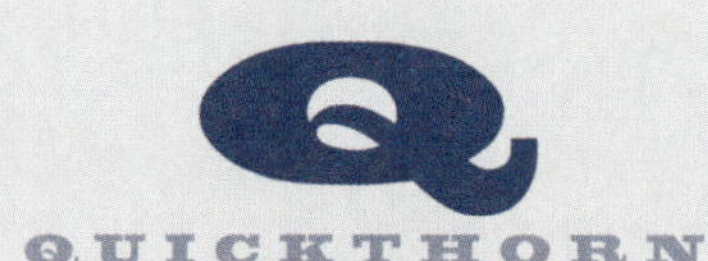

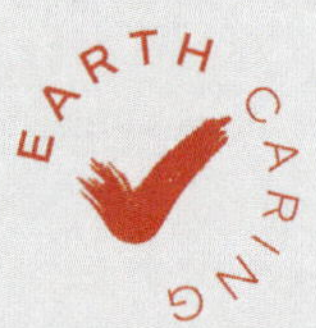

Collect Print Collage: Printing with Nature

Published by Quickthorn
info@quickthornbooks.com
www.quickthornbooks.com
@quickthornbooks

Publisher: Katy Bevan
Editor: Charlotte Abrahams
Cover design: Francesca Chalk
Book design: Megan Sheer
Printed in the UK by Short Run Press

Printed on FSC certified paper in the UK
A CIP catalogue record for this book is available from the British Library
ISBN 978-1-0683215-5-9